Today's philosophers may like to think of themselves as the culmination of a purposeful tradition going back two and a half millennia, but the record suggests something different: their predecessors were, for the most part, making their way along unmapped forest paths, with various combinations of ingenuity, frustration, anxiety, improvisation, frivolity and braggadocio. Instead of seeing their works as candidates for inclusion in some ultimate compendium of knowledge, we might do better to treat them as individual works of art forming a tradition as intricate and unpredictable as, say, Yoruba sculpture, Chinese poetry or the classical string quartet.

—Jonathan Rée, *from* Witcraft

Other Related Matters

Muindi Fanuel Muindi

SFPML

www.solutionsforpostmodernliving.org

First Printing, 2021

ISBN 978-0-578-93374-0

This book is dedicated to the memory of
MWATUM ZUBERI MUINDI
(1959-2009)

Table of Contents

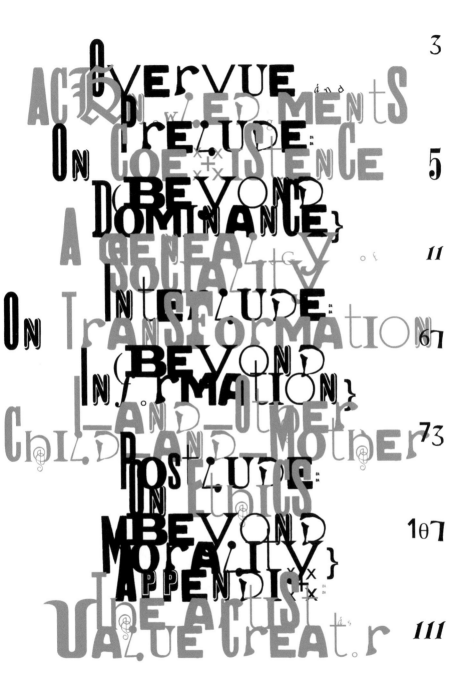

Overtue et Acknowledgments

My first three books, collected in the volume titled **TRIPTYCH**,
attempted to answer the question, "How do I become what I am?"
This book, my fourth, attempts to answer the immediate follow up question:
"Knowing how I become what I am, how do I relate to others?"

The two texts that form the core of this book approach the question of
"relating to others" from two different "logical" perspectives.
A Genealogy of Sociality, *approaches the question from*
a "sociological" perspective, attending to "social relations".
I-and-Other, Child-and-Mother *approaches the question from*
a "psychological" perspective, attending to "personal relations".
The terms "logical", "sociological", and "psychological" are placed
within quotation marks here because these terms only apply to my texts
metaphorically and ironically: I am not a legitimate heir to the disciplines
that have reduced these terms in order to make representative claims about reality.

I wrote the two texts at the core of this book in response to
the proceedings of two discussion groups that I organized and convened
during the height of the COVID-19 pandemic.
A Genealogy of Sociality *was written in response to the proceedings of*
the (ANTI-}SOCIAL (ANTI-}BODIES.
I-and-Other, Child-and-Mother *was written in response to the proceedings of*
the VIrULENT(LY} SELf(ISh}.
These two texts owe a great deal to the remarkable conversations that took place
in and around these two discussion groups, and I invite readers to review
the sprawling and ambitious proceedings of these two discussion groups
for themselves at solutionsforpostmodernliving.org.

Finally, I am glad to acknowledge and give thanks to
the friends and collaborators who graciously provided me with
kind comments, constructive criticisms, insightful questions,
and delightful suggestions as I put this book together.
Ylfa Muindi, Jonathan Agins, Niklas Damiris, Nathaniel Elias Mengist,
and Phillip Thurtle: I could not have written this book without you!

3

PRELUDE:

ON CO-EXISTENCE

(BEYOND DOMINANCE}

oNE.

An "authentic" learned behavior, or a whim,
is a behavior learned *without* reference to symbols and,
as such, it is a behavior that is invested with sentiments
but *not* invested with a logic.
By contrast, a "conventional" learned behavior, or a custom,
is a behavior learned *with* reference to symbols and,
as such, it is a behavior that is invested with a logic
in addition to being invested with sentiments.

two.

A culture is a group of interrelated and interdependent customs.
Or, in other words, a culture is a group of learned behaviors
that have been invested with a logic
by a group of interrelated and interdependent symbols.

THREE.

Different cultures come into conflict with one another when
(i) they invest similar learned behaviors with dissimilar logics, or
(ii) when they invest dissimilar learned behaviors with similar logics.
For example, a cultural conflict may arise for an individual because
this culture claims burping is a sign of rudeness and
teaches one to conceal one's burps as a logical consequence, while
that culture claims burping is a show of appreciation for a meal and
teaches one to make a show of burping as a consequence.
Another example, a cultural conflict may arise when two cultures
claim that one must revere one's superiors, but
this culture teaches that it is logical to tolerate rudeness
from one's superiors in a show of reverence, while
that culture teaches that it is logical to riposte rudeness
from one's superiors in a show of reverence.

One culture **dominates** *other cultures by making its own logic*
override and overrule the logic of others.
This is to say, in other words, that a dominant culture forces its own logic
on all learned behaviors,
overriding and overruling the alternative logics
that so-called "subcultures" give to learned behaviors.

F ?VE.

Instead of dominating other cultures, one culture **coexists** *with other cultures*
by compromising its own logic in order to accommodate the logic of others.
Coexisting cultures agree:
    (i) that a given learned behavior can be invested
    with many different logics,
    (ii) that no one logic for a given learned behavior can be objectively
    higher, nor truer, nor more desirable than any other, and
    (iii) that all logics ought to be compromised whenever and wherever
    cultural conflicts arise.

SI**X**.

Insofar as different logics for the same learned behavior may be mutually exclusive
and beyond rational arbitration, coexisting cultures negotiate conflicts
with appeals to **sentiments beyond reasons.**
Unlike logics, sentiments are never mutually exclusive:
differing sentiments can be superposed atop one another
and can coexist in superpositions.
Take, for instance, the bittersweet as a superposition of wonder and sadness,
or take the love-hate relationship that betrays superpositions of
love and cruelty.
Coexisting cultures resolve conflicts by deferring to the differing sentiments
of the persons involved in conflicts, thusly enabling
compromises that are unreasonable yet sensible,
compromises that conflicted parties can *feel* satisfied with
in spite of their logical contradictions.

SEVEN

Dominant cultures diminish and discredit subcultures
 by appealing to **reasons beyond sentiments.**
Logical arguments against sentimentality are the hallmarks
 of dominant cultures, and those who argue that there is
   "no room for sentiment" when it comes to resolving a conflict
    are arguing for cultural dominance
     as opposed to coexistence.
Dominant cultures disparage sentiments for *confusing* matters
 and esteem logics for *representing* matters clearly and distinctly.
Objecting to unreasonable compromises, dominant cultures "resolve"
 cultural conflicts by determining the higher logic
  that overrides and overrules all others,
   clearing the way for a reasonable compromise.

EIGHt.

A counterculture *is a subculture that resists a dominant culture*
 and that promotes cultural coexistence.
Countercultures negotiate cultural conflicts by frustrating higher logics,
 and by deferring to the differing sentiments of the parties to a conflict.
It is the would-be dominant culture that fights fire with fire,
 pitting one logic against another in order to discover which is
  the highest, truest, and most desirable.
Countercultures subvert logical arguments by situating them
 in sentimental stories, in narratives
  that characterize and contextualize logical contradictions.

NINE.

Sentimental storytelling *enables us to seek and discover compromises*
 that we can *feel* satisfied with in spite of their logical contradictions.
In doing so, sentimental stories distinguish themselves from didactic stories.
Whereas didactic stories betray sentiments to obey higher logics,
 sentimental stories betray logics in deference to differing sentiments.

7

tEN

Didacticism is part and parcel of displays of cultural dominance.
Sentimentalism is part and parcel of attempts at cultural coexistence.
If sentimentalism has a low reputation in our time, it is because
**so few of us still know how to express and interpret sentiments
with any skill and subtlety.**
When we condemn sentimentalism in storytelling,
we are like the failed painter turned photographer who cites his own lack
of painterly skill (and his facility for photography)
when claiming that portrait painting is a lower artform
than portrait photography.
Sentimental storytelling is not a low artform in and of itself, rather,
it is a low artform when those who practice it have little or no skill for it.

ELeVeN.

Dominant cultures endeavor to stifle and suppress
the development of skills for sentimental storytelling
in order to ensure that sentimentalism cannot be deployed
by countercultures against dominant cultures.
The retainers of dominant cultures, their bureaucrats and their soldiers,
mustn't be allowed to fall prey to sentimentalisms
that would keep them from executing their duties as retainers.
To this end, dominant cultures take efforts to devalue sentimentalism
so that sentiments come to seem trite, cloying, and impotent
relative to the "facts of life" and the "power of logic".
The fall of sentimental storytelling
and the concomitant ascent of information gathering and reporting
are not historical accidents that have befallen our time.
**The art of sentimental storytelling has been pushed to new lows
and the science of information gathering and reporting
has been carried to new heights
by cultures bent on achieving dominance.**
It should be no wonder that the rise of capitalism and colonialism
as highly refined techniques of cultural dominance
involved the proliferation of information technologies
and the decimation of storytelling traditions.
Ay, and it is no wonder that the dominant cultures of our time tell us that,
the gathering and reporting of information has become essential and
storytelling is nothing but a diversion or an ornamentation.

TWELVE.

To promote cultural coexistence, it is imperative that
    the art of storytelling and its attendant sentimentalism
        be revived, refreshed, and provisioned to outmaneuver and outwit
            the didacticism that attends the science of information
                gathering and reporting.
Those who would fight for **a multicultural world,**
    and who would fight against the spread of a global monoculture,
        must recognize that a multicultural world is a world rife
            with cultural conflicts that will need to be resolved
                with the aid of sentimental storytelling.
This is to say, in other words, that a multicultural world
    is a world in which storytelling becomes an essential practice
        that precedes, exceeds, and succeeds the gathering and reporting
            of information.

A GENE_ALOGY of SOCIALI_TY

Man is by nature a social animal; an individual who is unsocial naturally and not accidentally is either beneath our notice or more than human. Society is something that precedes the individual. Anyone who either cannot lead the common life or is so self-sufficient as not to need to, and therefore does not partake of society, is either a beast or a god.
— Aristotle *from* Politics

Introduction

The Stakes

It is the 21st Century of the Common Era, *roughly three hundred millennia since the species H. sapiens emerged from a predecessor within the genus Homo, roughly a hundred millennia since H. sapiens equipped with symbolic social forms began migrating out of Africa, roughly ten millennia since H. sapiens first domesticated plants and animals, roughly five millennia since H. sapiens developed formal writing and the first "exact" predictive sciences, roughly two centuries since H. sapiens began to exploit fossil fuels at an industrial scale, roughly a century since H. sapiens split the atom, and roughly a half century since H. sapiens deciphered the genetic code and set foot on the surface of the moon.*

Life is in a process of breaking down, of cracking up: half the world's wildlife is gone, half the world's forests, half the world's topsoil. Meanwhile, derivative fascisms* are proliferating: "there's always another attack, election, coup, or someone upping the ante in terms of violence, misogyny, snuff, or infamy."

Whatever could have happened for things to have come to this? Everyone knows that something remarkable and terrifying must have happened, but few have a positive sense or understanding of what. All are certain that this remarkable and terrifying happening was a social *event, having to do with the artifice or nature of* sociality, *but the most alluring diagnoses regarding the origins of our present situation all account for much less than what they purport to.*

---

* *Hito Steyerl coined the term "derivative fascisms" in an essay on "Contemporary Art and Derivative Fascisms". In this essay, Steyerl writes, "The term 'derivative fascisms' means a jumble of widespread extreme right-wing movements that relate to twentieth-century fascisms in terms of future options, but not by any means as equivalents, as in: creating and marketing future options for fascism. There is no point in asking whether they are really fascisms or not because fascism is the underlying entity, which may or may not have anything to do with its derivatives."*

11

A Genealogy of Sociality

Our Genealogy of Sociality *aims to develop a diagnosis that could both account for more than others and rival the allure of others. Ostensibly, this essay is a diagnosis of origins, recognizing that the term "diagnosis" is derived from the Greek* diagignōskein *"to know apart (from another)" and that the term "origin" is derived from the Latin* oriri *"to rise; appear over the horizon". That being said, putting literal matters aside and focusing on literary matters, this essay should be read like a novella. Two French philosophers, Gilles Deleuze and Felix Guattari, once proposed that the novella was a literary genre organized around the question, "What happened? Whatever could have happened?" But they also proposed that "the novella has little to do with a memory of the past or an act of reflection; quite to the contrary, it plays upon a fundamental forgetting." Our* Genealogy of Sociality *proceeds from the assumption that whatever could have happened has been forgotten and has to be re-collected or, rather more precisely, that whatever could have happened had to have happened unknowingly and has to be re-constructed from scant traces and by way of thought experiments. At the same time, however, our essay also assumes that whatever could have happened can neither be properly re-collected nor properly re-constructed because it wasn't a conventional historical happening. Indeed, our essay assumes a* para-historical *happening, a betrayal of the form, function, and structure of conventional historical happenings. Ay, and in so far as the novella is the side-story* [para-histoire] *that betrays the form, function, and structure of the conventional chronicle of happenings* [histoire événementielle], *our* Genealogy of Sociality *is to a conventional history of sociality what the novella is to the conventional chronicle of happenings.*

Introduction

More profoundly still, this essay should be read like a novella because this essay owes a great deal more to creative imagination than it does to analytical and empirical investigation. This fact follows, in part, from all that was already stated above: because that which cannot be properly re-collected or re-constructed has to be re-imagined in a (re-)creative manner. Going further, this fact also follows from whom we, the genealogists, are. We are neither "academic authorities" nor "scientific researchers". We are what Augusto Boal would call "spect-actors". *We are spectators-and-actors in the para-historical happening that we have endeavored to re-imagine in this essay. This is to say, in other words, that we are not, nor do we pretend to be, disinterested parties. On the contrary, as the sometimes denizens of* Western "Educated", Industrialized, Rich, and "Democratic" (WEiRD} *nations and cosmopolitan "global cities", we are interested and involved parties. We are aware of the fact that our own imaginations will be implicated in whatever could have happened, and we are aware of the fact that explicating whatever could have happened will, in part, be a matter of explicating what we have imagined into being. Indeed, the implication of the imagination in whatever could have happened is precisely that which makes whatever could have happened a para-historical happening as opposed to conventional historical one: for that which has been imagined into being is precisely that which cannot be re-collected or re-constructed but can only be re-imagined in a (re-)creative manner. Thus, our* Genealogy *is, in the last instance, organized around the question, "Whatever could have happened in and to our imaginations for things to have come to this?"*

A Genealogy of Sociality

Born black in New York City in the late 1980s to a broken middle-class immigrant family hailing from the depths of the East African Rift Valley, a dropout and autodidact, working as a lowly administrator at a public university on the Pacific Northwest Coast of the United States, and lacking the meritocratic credentials that would authorize me to make a legitimate diagnosis of the human condition, I convened the (ANTI-)SOCIAL (ANTI-)BODIES during the summer of 2020 in spite of who I was. It was the turn of my thirty-third year, and I was suffering under the "new global monasticism" effected by the all-too-necessary social distancing measures and stay-at-home orders adopted to fight the COVID-19 pandemic. The spread of COVID-19 had sparked a global public health crisis. Uneven global responses to this public health crisis had sparked a global economic crisis. Uneven responses to this economic crisis were exacerbating ongoing political and cultural crises that had already rattled the (neo)liberal West and destabilized a global capitalist "order of things" that depended upon (neo)liberal political institutions and cultural practices. By many accounts, I was a probable victim of these cascading crises, and my knowing or not knowing their origins was a superfluous matter. I was to be a statistic, at worst, or, at best, a case study, leaving behind some scant trace of myself that would inform the thought experiments of a better credentialed and more analytical or empirical mind. In no way was I, Muindi Fanuel Muindi, authorized to act as a clinician of the human condition.

But by my own account, however superfluous it was, I had not yet become the victim of whatever had happened. By my own account, I could still survive and thrive in spite of whatever had happened, but I could only do so if I had a diagnosis of the human condition that I could handle and play to some advantage. Having found no diagnosis that I could play to any advantage, I needed to develop a diagnosis for myself and to do so as quickly as possible, lest I perish. I had to urgently ask and answer the question, "What happened?" Under no pretense was I entitled to ask and answer the question, but asking and answering the question seemed a matter of life and death to me, and I refused to let a lack of credentials prematurely sentence me to death.

Thankfully, I rightly figured that this question was a matter of life and death for others like and unlike me, some credentialed and some uncredentialed, some more analytical, some more empirical, some more imaginative. Knowing better than to go it alone, I put out a call for others who had no choice but to ask and answer the question, inviting them to join me in the asking and the answering. The unconventional artists, writers, and thinkers who joined with me in the asking and the answering formed the (ANTI-)SOCIAL (ANTI-)BODIES.

The (ANTI-)SOCIAL (ANTI-)BODIES *embarked upon a* Genealogy of Sociality *collectively, but this essay is my own idiosyncratic impression of the results of our endeavors. I must make use of a "we" in this text because I cannot claim the thoughts articulated in this text for myself alone. The reader ought to recognize, however, that the "we" in this text is highly diffracted and refracted by me. In no way does this text purport to be an accurate reflection of the "we" that it presumes. Rather, this text is a warped reflection, a primitivist rendering of the* (ANTI-)SOCIAL (ANTI-)BODIES, *akin to Picasso's rendering of* Les Demoiselles d'Avignon. *It is my hope that the others who participated in the endeavor will someday offer up their own reflections and that their reflections will bear little resemblance to mine.*

Ay, so, presuming to speak for my fellow travelers, a brief summary of our diagnosis runs as follows:

A new and more virulent strain of the human condition emerged between the fifteenth and nineteenth centuries of the Common Era, and was incubated in regions of the world that had been colonized by Western European nation–states and their forerunners. In the wake of three World Wars during the twentieth century, two "hot wars" and one "cold war", this new and more virulent strain of the human condition conquered the entire globe. This new strain of the human condition not only threatens to obliterate the animal in the human but, more profoundly, it threatens to obliterate the animal in general.

Indulge me, if you will, and try to understand the term "animal" here in the broadest possible sense, invoking the Latin animale *"living being, being which breathes", from* anima *"breath, soul; a current of air", but also invoking the* animisms *that find all beings inspired and inspiring, including mineral, vegetal, and elemental beings alongside those beings that we commonly call animals. Stretching the term to its most tenuous extreme, try to understand that the term "animal" here refers to any inspired or inspiring being, to any being that is in some sense aerial, aerated, atmospheric, breathable or breathing.*

Was it only a coincidence that we came to such a diagnosis in the midst of the COVID-19 pandemic which was needlessly taking the breath away from millions? Was it only a coincidence that we came to such a diagnosis in the wake of the protests in response to the murder of George Floyd, who died breathless while pinned under the knee of a police officer? Was it only a coincidence that we came to such a diagnosis as we breathed in air that contained greater concentrations of carbon dioxide than ever before in human history as a result of human activity? Being a Black African in America, one lacking higher credentials and making ends meet by performing bullshit and soon-to-be-automated forms of administrative labor: this diagnosis only made me more keenly aware of the fact that I am so easily taken for a less than human beast by the powers that be, making me into a probable victim of this more virulent strain of the human condition. In other words, I am statistically less likely to be treated "humanely" by the powers that be and, thus, I am more likely to perish during a pandemic, more likely to be slain by an "officer of the peace", and more likely to be the victim of some climate injustice. Perhaps this diagnosis is but an echo of the last words of Eric Garner, Javier Ambler, Manuel Ellis, Elijah McClain, and George Floyd,

"I CAN'T BREATHE."

INTRODUCTION

Our diagnosis contrasts the term "animal" with the term "human", the latter of which is etymologically derived from Proto-Indo-European *(dh)ghomon–, making the human being, literally, an "earthling" or earthly being. Contrasted with the inspired or inspiring animal, the human is hum-bled and hum-bling, hum-iliated and hum-iliating. The perilous new human condition that we have diagnosed is the condition of being "human, all too human" and hostile to the animal, being "earthly, all too earthly" and hostile to the sky, being so humbled and so humiliated that one can no longer inspire or be inspired by others. That being said, however, we do not mean to suggest that the human is necessarily hostile to the animal, nor that the earth is necessarily hostile to the sky, nor that humbleness and humility are necessarily hostile to inspiration. Our diagnosis, rather, finds that the symbol is responsible for this new strain of humanity which seeks dispense with the animal, this new strain of the earth which seeks to suffocate the sky, this new strain of humbleness and humility which seeks to smother inspiration.

It is widely held that the human species is distinguished from other species by being the only known "symbolic species", the only species that regards the use and abuse of symbols as a matter of life-and-death. We would like to suggest that, in addition to being that which distinguished the human species from others, the rise of the symbol was also the para-historical happening that introduced the break between earth and sky, human and animal, body and breath. It is the symbol that pits one against the other, that divides and conquers. Dividing the earth from the sky but favoring neither one in or for itself, the symbol employs whichever one is ready-to-hand to quash the other. While the "human, all too human" condition in our age is defined by the symbol's use of the earth to suffocate the sky, in the age prior to ours, the "human, all too human" condition had been defined by the symbol's use of the sky to swallow the earth.

A GENEALOGY Of SOCIALITY

Prior to the emergence of the symbol, neither earth nor sky, neither human nor animal, neither body nor breath existed in and of themselves: there was only the horizon, *the *singular confusion* of earth-and-sky, human-and-animal, body-and-breath. Ay, and what the symbol seeks is not the obliteration of earth or sky but, rather, the obliteration of the horizon, either by making the earth suffocate the sky or, vice versa, by making the sky swallow the earth. Indeed, we become "human, all too human" whenever we come to believe either that the sky must swallow the earth or that the earth must suffocate the sky, whenever we come to believe that the human-and-animal horizon must be obliterated, that the human can do in and do without the animal.*

If our diagnosis of our present strikes you as no more than a preposterous play on words, I would suggest that you stop reading here and that you consider whether your desire for a diagnosis in grounded literal terms, as opposed to soaring literary terms, is an indication that your humanity is well on its way to obliterating your animality. On the other hand, if our diagnosis strikes you as a meaningful play on words, however minimally, please read on, for there is more to this diagnosis than there might seem upon first reading. For one thing, in spite of all that was said above, the symbol is not to be repudiated and obliterated in order to rescue the horizon. The definitive victory of the horizon over the symbol seems to us no more desirable than the definitive victory of the symbol over the horizon. In the game of Go, the term Seki (セキ) refers to an impasse that cannot be resolved into simple life or death for either side. This term is often translated as "mutual life". Our diagnosis revolves around a kindred notion of "mutual life": our concern is for a way to achieve "mutual life" for the symbol-and-horizon, as opposed to life for one and death for the other.

Many readers might now be asking themselves, "This is all well and good, but what has all this to do with sociality?" Well, we hold that the human–and–animal horizon is sociality itself. *We hold that all social species live on the human-and-animal horizon, not just our so-called human species, H. sapiens.*

Introduction

Is it any wonder that all animals strike us as human when we can "relate to them" socially, when we observe them conspiring and when they inspire social sentiments in us? We hold that H. sapiens is a social species first and a symbolic species second, and that our symbolic capacities are an outgrowth of our social capacities. In other words, we hold that the symbol first emerged as an implication of the human-and-animal horizon and that it has explicated the horizon in addition to threatening the horizon with obliteration.

The symbol's explicative capacity relative to the horizon has always been attended by an obliterative capacity, but we hold that the symbol has become a threat to the horizon only since humans started to identify as human first and foremost, rather than a species of social animal. Whatever could have happened to have made such a vulgar claim, "human(ity) first", possible? Our **Genealogy** *will follow the symbol's development, from implication of the horizon, to explication of the horizon, to the obliteration of the horizon, in order to reveal how the symbol's development betrays and is betrayed by the horizon in and through the claim "human(ity) first". Indeed, if you will allow us to appropriate some figures from the thought of the German philosopher Friedrich Nietzsche, our narrative will reveal that it is the* **Last Man** *who believes that "putting humanity first" is the secret to happiness. "Formerly all the world was insane", — say the subtlest of them, and blink thereby. Meanwhile, the* **Beyond–Human** *is inspired by the human who keeps company with the eagle who soars across the sky and the serpent who slithers along the earth, and, what's more, the* **Beyond–Human** *inspires the human to protest against the scourge that would forever transform an animal into a dull beast.**

---

* *It should be noted that we shall appropriate a number of figures from the thought of Nietzsche throughout this text. For instance, Nietzsche's* **Genealogy of Morality** *provided us with the idea for a genealogy that owes more to creative imagination than to documentary investigation, very unlike a history. Furthermore, and more profoundly still, our philosophical cosmology of the symbol-and-horizon takes a great deal from Nietzsche's philosophical cosmology. That being said, however, we do not feel beholden to Nietzsche nor his work in any way whatsoever, in spite of all that we have taken from him. As Igor Stravinsky once put it, "good composers borrow, great composers steal." The borrower cannot do what they will with what they have taken because the borrower wants to return what they have taken to its rightful owner in tact. The thief, having broken the chain of rightful ownership, can do what they will with what they have taken. We have stolen from Nietzsche, and we fancy ourselves thieves in the mold of Robin Hood and his Merry Men: stealing from the rich and giving to the poor. The rich may elegantly look down upon the coarse and graceless needs and distresses of us poor folk, but we poor folk know how to make good use of what we manage to steal from the rich. All that we have stolen from Nietzsche will be put to poor use in this text, yes, but this is not a flaw but, rather, a feature of this text.*

A genealogy of Sociality

We have re-imagined the story of the symbol and its relation to the horizon in six chapters. These chapters run as follows:

- In the first chapter, **the Horizon**, we have re-imagined the rise of symbol on the human-and-animal horizon.

- In the second chapter, **Kindred Spirits**, we have re-imagined human-and-animal socialities, in the light of the rise of the symbol, as socialities revolving around communing with "kindred spirits" (i.e., beings beside human beings that populate the horizon).

- In the third chapter, **Minor Gods**, we have re-imagined how the symbol explicated human-and-animal socialities to yield profane-and-sacred socialities: the latter being socialities that revolve around emulating "Minor Gods" (i.e., beings above human beings that serve as role models).

- In the fourth chapter, **Major Gods**, we have re-imagined how the symbol explicated profane-and-sacred socialities to yield leisured-and-laboring socialities: the latter being socialities that revolve around the whims of "Major Gods"(i.e., beings above and beyond human beings that do not serve as role models but are served as whimsical rulers).

- In the fifth chapter, **The Absolute**, we have re-imagined how the symbol explicated leisured-and-laboring socialities to yield idealistic-and-materialistic socialities: the latter being socialities that revolve around the logic of the "Absolute" (i.e., a being [or a nothingness] that encompasses all beings, both human and non-human, not serving as a role model but being served as a rational, rather than whimsical, ruler).

- Finally, in the sixth chapter, **Statistics**, we have re-imagined how the symbol explicated idealistic-and-materialistic socialities to yield statistical-and-spectral socialities: the latter being socialities that revolve around inferring the rational will of a people (i.e., a population of human beings) by surveying/surveilling the irrational whims of persons (i.e., [in-]dividual human beings)

The fifth and sixth chapters are the decisive chapters of our **Genealogy**. *The fifth chapter re-imagines how the symbol pivoted away from explicating the horizon and began threatening the horizon by proposing that the sky swallow the earth. The sixth chapter re-imagines the decisive maneuvers that have enabled the symbol to make more dire threats against the horizon by proposing that the earth suffocate the sky.* But where the danger is, also grows the saving power. *The very same maneuvers that have enabled the symbol to pose a threat to the horizon have also enabled the symbol to explicate the horizon in more respects and with more respect than ever before. The fact that the symbol serves as a* **pharmakon***, a poison-and-remedy, with respect to the horizon cannot be underestimated. This is why, although they are not the decisive chapters, the first four chapters set the stage for the decisive fifth and sixth chapters in the most crucial way by demonstrating how the obliterative capacities of the symbol betray its explicative capacities.*

With that, we are now ready to proceed with our **Genealogy***, save for one last statement of intent. On the one hand, our* **Genealogy** *is only interested in finding out what happened: it is not at all interested in foretelling what is going to happen next. That being said, on the other hand, our* **Genealogy** *clearly knows what it does and does not want to happen next: it does not want the symbol to obliterate the horizon for good but it does want the symbol to continue to explicate the horizon in more respects and with more respect. This is to say, in other words, that our* **Genealogy** *has been written for the sake of those who would regard the horizon with ever increasing respect. We hope that our* **Genealogy** *manages to find those for the sake of whom it was written and that they find it inspired and inspiring.*

CHAPTER ONE

tHE HOr'Z.N

"In the beginning there was the Word..." *A preposterous proposition!*
For it was in the midst of things, in media res, *that the word or, more*
precisely, the symbol arose. In other words, the symbol first appeared
on the horizon, betwixt earth-and-sky, human-and-animal, body-and-
breath.

And yet, it is true that the rise of the symbol on the horizon marked
a certain beginning. For with the rise of the symbol on the horizon, the
singular confusion that constituted the horizon began to yield dualities:
earth-and-sky became earth on one side and sky on the other; human-
and-animal became human on one side and animal on the other;
body-and-breath became body on one side and breath on the other. And
these dualities, in turn, yielded the three most fundamental of all logics:
(i) the logic of extremes on a continuum (e.g., "it is human at one end
and animal at the other"); (ii) the logic of revolving cycles (e.g., "it is
by turns human and then animal"); and (iii) the logic of dichotomies
(e.g., "it is either human or animal").

It would be "ideal" if we could give you a straightforward, "In
the beginning there was..." account of the first appearance of the
symbol on the horizon. Alas, we cannot, as that would involve using
the symbol to account for the horizon that precedes, exceeds, and
succeeds it. So, instead, we will begin our account in media res, *we*
will use flashbacks and flash-forwards, and our narrative will be a
non-linear one. What's more, we will have to recognize that, in and
by all accounts, the symbol mis-represents the horizon by impressing
a logic onto it, by making the horizon appear to be either continuous,
circuitous, or dichotomous. It is crucial that we do not forget that,
in spite of all representations to the contrary, the horizon is neither
continuous, nor circuitous, nor dichotomous. Rather, the horizon is
the indeterminate substrate that precedes, exceeds, and succeeds all
continuities, circuits, and dichotomies.

A GENEALOGY OF SOCIALITY

We admit that this is singularly confusing, yes, but do not despair. What we are trying to say, quite simply, is that words can and will betray us throughout our Genealogy. Our account of the first appearance of the symbol on the horizon and our account of the subsequent development of the symbol relative to the horizon, will be suffused with metaphors and ironies. Indeed, we really ought to begin our Genealogy by acknowledging that our use of the term "horizon" is ironic and that our use of the term "symbol" is metaphorical.

First, let us take the term "horizon", from the Greek horizein which means "to bound, limit, divide, separate". You will no doubt note that throughout this text we will *NOT* be using the term horizon to refer to that which bounds, limits, divides, or separates earth from sky, human from animal, body from breath. Instead, ironically, we will use the term "horizon" to refer to the singular confusion, the mixing and melding of earth-and-sky, of human-and-animal, of body-and-breath. Why have we deployed the term "horizon" ironically? Well, because there is no way that the symbol, which can only approach matters dualistically, can un-ironically refer to the singular confusion that precedes, exceeds, and succeeds the rise of the symbol. Knowing this and not wanting to torture language in order to maintain the false pretense of proper terms, we have chosen to revel in irony. What's more, we believe that our use of term "horizon" is akin to kintsugi (金継ぎ, "golden joinery"). With the term "horizon", we split matters in two but we also rejoin matters again by defining the "horizon" using so many conjunctive phrases ("earth-and-sky", "human-and-animal", "body-and-breath"), phrases that highlight, rather than disguise, the splitting-and-rejoining process that characterizes our use the symbol to ironically refer to the singular confusion that is the symbol's condition of possibility. We readily admit that this is a sophistry, and we apologize for it. Still, we beg you to bear with us, for we believe that this sophistry will bare and bear all. What is most important for us is not that you understand our usage of the term "horizon" but that you get a feel for the rhythms of our usage.

CHAPTER ONE

Now, let us take the term "symbol". In this text, the term symbol will refer to the duality of the split on one side and the rejoined on the other: this as opposed to the singularly confused "split-and-rejoined" term "horizon" from the paragraph above. To get a better idea of what we mean by "symbol", we ask that you consider that the term "symbol" is derived from the Ancient Greek term symbolon, *referring to a thing that had been broken into fitting pieces to register and remember an affinity. As David Graeber writes in* Debt: The First 5,000 Years:

Two friends at dinner might create a symbolon if they took some object—a ring, a knucklebone, a piece of crockery—and broke it in half. Any time in the future when either of them had need of the other's help, they could bring their halves as reminders of the friendship. Archaeologists have found hundreds of little broken friendship tablets of this sort in Athens, often made of clay. Later they became ways of sealing a contract, the object standing in the place of witnesses. The word was also used for tokens of every sort: those given to Athenian jurors entitling them to vote, or tickets for admission to the theater. It could be used to refer to money too, but only if that money had no intrinsic value: bronze coins whose value was fixed only by local convention. Used for written documents, a symbolon could also be passport, contract, commission, or receipt. By extension, it came to mean: omen, portent, symptom, or finally, in the now-familiar sense, *symbol*.

Throughout this text the symbol will be regarded as a means of registering and remembering affinities via the splitting of the horizon (earth-and-sky, human-and-animal, body-and-breath) into fitting pieces (earth on one side and sky on the other, human on one side and animal on the other, body on one side and breath on the other) which may be rejoined, again and again, over the course of time. Ay, and our succeeding account of the development of the symbol will be an account of affinities registered, remembered and, perhaps most importantly, betrayed by the symbol

A GENEALOGY OF SOCIALITY

So, to recap: when earth-and-sky became earth on one side and sky on the other, when human-and-animal became human on one side and animal on the other, when body-and-breath became body on one side and breath on the other—we hold that these splittings first, foremost, and above all else, registered and remembered affinities. Here, in this first chapter of our Genealogy, we shall re-imagine the circumstances that gave rise to the desire or need for affinities to be registered and remembered by symbolon, by splittings into fitting pieces that go their own separate ways for a time only to be rejoined together again and again, time after time.

Indulge us if you will and imagine a fission–fusion society: a society whose members go their own separate ways for a time (e.g., foraging individually or in small groups during the day) only to rejoin one another again and again, time after time.(e.g., sleeping in larger groups every night). With this image in mind, it should be no wonder that the symbol arose within the fission-fusion societies of a certain social animal, as the image of fission–fusion society evokes our earlier description symbol. And yet, it is clearly the case that a fission-fusion society is, at best, only a necessary condition for the symbol to arise and not a sufficient condition: there are many species lineages that are characterized by fission-fusion societies but there is only one known lineage, our own, which lives-and-dies by its use-and-abuse of the symbol. In other words, fission-fusion only facilitates the rise of the symbol, it does not necessitate the symbol's rise.

We imagine that the sufficient conditions for the rise of the symbol have something specific to do with "times-at-which" members of fission-fusion societies went their separate ways, on one side, and, on the other side, with the "times-over-the-course-of-which" members of fission-fusion societies joined together again and again. Yet, for the first time but not the last, we find ourselves implying that symbolic logics apply to a matter that precedes, exceeds, and succeeds symbolic logics. We have just implied the logic of extremes of a continuum: members of a society being forever separated on one extreme and being forever together on the other. We have also just implied the logic of turns of a cycle: members of a society being by turns separated from one another and rejoined together. Last but not least, we have also implied the logic of dichotomization: members of a society being either separated from one another or joined together at any given time.

To avoid these logical implications, let us state clearly that, instead of imagining that there was a fundamental logic at work in fission-fusion societies that gave rise of the symbol, we are imagining that the experience of living in a fission-fusion society is the pre-logical experience that the symbol formalizes and turns into logics. In other words, the experience of fission-fusion sociality is the symbol's condition of possibility. All fission-fusion societies split the horizon in two and rejoin it, and the symbol is but the generalization of such splittings and rejoinings. Ay, and it follows from this that the central question for us is this: what were the ecological, ethological, and aesthetic conditions that made it desirable for H. sapiens to formalize the experience of splitting the horizon in two and rejoining it?

Getting back to our point, we imagine that the rise of the symbol has something specific to do with the relation between the "times-at-which" members of societies go their separate ways, on one side, and, on the other side, the "times-over-the-course-of-which" members of societies join together again and again. Indeed, putting all our cards on the table: we imagine this "something specific" was a desire or need for an augmented "pathos of distance" that is, to borrow some language from the French semiotician Roland Barthes, "a distance that won't destroy affect [...] a distance permeated, irrigated by tender feeling: a pathos that would allow for something of Eros [affection] and Sophia [discernment]."

Approaching this problem from a different angle: the problem with being separate on one side and together on the other side was, in the first instance, an "aesthetic" problem. We are using the term "aesthetic" here in its dual sense as having to do with "time and distance", on the one side, and having to do with "matters of sentiment", on the other side. When members of a society are separated and must wander apart without each other's company for any span of time, members of a society can become less and less sensitive to each other's sentiments over time insofar as their sentiments can come to differ over time. This is a problem because being together with others socially means nothing other than having a sense for one another's sentiments and this, in turn, means that being apart for longer and longer spans of time can diminish being together socially and can cause our sociality to atrophy.

A Genealogy of Sociality

We imagine that the aesthetic problem we have described above became an ethological and ecological problem when evolving circumstances were such that individual H. sapiens sentiments became more and more liable to change rapidly over time while, at the same time, H. sapiens were being compelled to spend longer and longer spans of time apart before joining together again. In response to these evolving circumstances, in order to remain social, H. sapiens cultivated symbolic capacities as a means to achieve an augmented "pathos of distance", as a means for H. sapiens to rapidly regain a sense for one another's sentiments after having been kept at a distance for increasingly long spans of time. Consider this for a moment: is it any wonder that we spend so much time using symbols to communicate our likes and dislikes, our similarities and differences, and the ways in which our sentiments have changed over time? Consider this as well: are we ever more thankful for the symbol than when we have the opportunity to catch up with distant friends and relations, to tell each other stories about experiences that we have had without one another, and to discuss how our experiences have made us differ over time?

Yet, at the same time, we ought to consider the fact that the symbol can only enable us to communicate things that differ about us over the course of time by making things about us seem to repeat time after time. In other words, the symbol creates the appearance of repetitions about us in order to enable the communication of differences amongst us. This is not to say, however, that the symbol actually makes things about us repeat time after time. Rather, to be clear, this is only to say that the symbol makes it *seem* as if things about us repeat time after time.

Now, we imagine that, at first, the times during which H. sapiens needed a symbolically augmented pathos of distance were rare: that it was initially rare for H. sapiens to spend great spans of time apart before coming together again. That being said, however, we also imagine that the times that called for a symbolically augmented pathos of distance, however rare, were remarkably important times, and given the importance of such times, however rare, it would be important for H. sapiens to practice with the symbol in preparation for such times. In the next chapter, we will imagine the ways in which H. sapiens practiced with the symbol in preparation for rare but important times that called for a symbolically augmented pathos of distance.

CHAPTER TWO

How can we **WEɪRD**-lings, the denizens of the enclaves of Western-"**E**ducated", ɪndustrialized, **R**ich, and "**D**emocratic" cultures, possibly (re-)imagine life in a primitive* society? How can we (re-)imagine a life that is neither continuous, nor circuitous, nor dichotomous, a life defined by its indeterminateness rather than a determinate logic that has been impressed upon it by the symbol? The logics of the symbol are part and parcel of **WEɪRD** processes of making bread and butter, and we **WEɪRD**-lings can hardly nourish ourselves without them. For us, a symbolic discredit means life or death, and we find it difficult to imagine how it could be otherwise. Difficult, yes, but not impossible, for there was a time in all our lives during which such logics could not define us. Indeed, let us take a poet's advice here and remember our childhoods, "marvelous, lavish source[s], treasure-hood[s] of memories". We must, of course, recognize that our **WEɪRD** childhoods were, in large part, training for **WEɪRD** adulthoods defined by symbolic logics, but we must also recognize that, as children, we often imagined and longed for a primitive adulthood that lacked a defining logic. Indeed, although we have trained for **WEɪRD** adulthoods and have learned to deny our childish longings for primitive adulthoods, we can remember and draw inspiration from our childish longings in order to (re-)creatively re-imagine what a primitive adulthood for ourselves.

Primitive societies, as we began to imagine them in the last chapter, rarely needed a symbolically augmented pathos of distance to maintain sociality. Yet, however rare this need was, we imagine it was still an important need. As such, primitive societies made sure to practice with the symbol in preparation for the rare but important times that asked for a symbolically augmented pathos of distance. That being said, however, we do not imagine that their practice was a serious practice intended to make perfect nor do we imagine that it was a playful practice for idle times. Indeed, avoiding the trap of assuming a duality, we will reject the idea that there is playful practice here and serious practice there, and, we will instead imagine the singular confusion of playful-and-serious practice.

---

* The term "primitive" is from the Latin primitivus "first or earliest of its kind", from primitus "at first", from primus "first". We will be using the term "primitive" throughout this text in spite of the unfortunate connotations that the term has acquired. We hold that the term primitive can only be used as a pejorative by adherents of a progressivism that claims humanity first and that disclaims the primitive for being human-and-animal. Advocates of a primitivism that puts the human-and-animal first must (re-)claim the "primitive" as a term of endearment.

A GENEALOGY OF SOCIALITY

Have you ever watched young children practicing with symbols?
Have you noticed how young children are always making splits
regarding what should be taken seriously and what should be taken
lightly? Have you noticed how young children do not take such splits for
granted even after they have been made? Have you noticed how young
children assume that all splits fade and blur over time and have to
continually be remade again and again if they are to be re-used again
and again? Have you noticed how the young child considers it rude to
take playfulness or seriousness for granted? When the WEiRD adult takes
playfulness or seriousness for granted, the young child protests, "How
was I supposed to know that you were being serious? How was I
supposed to know that you were only kidding?" To do right by the child
is to recognize that the distinction between the playful and the serious
has to be (re-)created, again and again from a substrate which is both
playful-and-serious.

We would endeavor to re-imagine all that we have noticed the above
in a more profound way with respect to primitive social life, speaking
in terms of the **profane** *and the* **sacred** *in addition to the playful and*
the serious. Primitives, as we imagine them, take neither the profane
nor the sacred for granted. Rather, primitives maintain the existence
of a **preternatural** *profane-and-sacred horizon. Primitive symbolic*
practices split-and-rejoin this preternatural horizon so as to yield
profane natures on one side and sacred supernaturals on the other, but
only for a time and not for all time. The primitive believes that such
splits should never taken for granted, and when such a split is taken
for granted, the primitive protests, "How rudely you assume that the
profane is profane and the sacred is sacred? Sacred things and profane
things are not given things. They are, rightly, things made different for a
time, that can only made different via the splitting of the preternatural
profane-and-sacred horizon that precedes, exceeds and succeeds them.
What's more the difference between the profane and the sacred fades
and blurs over time and has to be remade again and again if it is to be
re-used again and again."

CHAPTER TWO

The preternatural profane-and-sacred horizon, is the very horizon of conventions-and-sentiments whose existence we implied at the end of the last chapter. Recall that the symbol only enables us to communicate things that differ about us as time passes by making things about us appear to repeat time after time. Things that are sacred are things that differ about us as time passes: our private sentiments (or our "whims"). Things that are profane are things about us that seem to repeat time and time again: shared conventions (or "customs"). The symbol splits conventions from sentiments but only for a time. The split fades and blurs after a time into the singular confusion of conventions-and-sentiments that precedes, exceeds, and succeeds the split.

Indeed, as we imagine it, the human-and-animal horizon, the profane-and-sacred horizon, the horizon of conventions-and-sentiments are one and the same horizon. It follows that we may rephrase the primitive's protest against the assumption of dualities as follows, "How rudely you assume that a human is a human and an animal is an animal, that conventions are conventional and sentiments are sentimental? Humans and animals, conventions and sentiments: these are not givens. They are, rightly, made different for a time, but they can only made different via the splitting of the horizon that precedes, exceeds and succeeds any and every split: the human-and-animal, the conventional-and-sentimental. What's more the differences between human and animal, conventional and sentimental, fade and blur over time and they have to be remade time and time again if they are to be used time and time again."

Insofar as we are aware of and involved in the lives of other social animals, we who are not rude, who are not "human, all too human" must, rightly, regard and respect the horizon—the human-and-animal, the conventional-and-sentimental, the profane-and-sacred—as all social animals populate this horizon. In other words, those of us who are not rude must, rightly, regard and respect other species, symbolic or not, as "kindred spirits", as preternatural beings populating the horizon of conventions-and-sentiments. What's more, insofar as the social life of humans is not entirely defined by the symbol and its logics, humans must also, rightly, regard and respect one another as preternatural beings populating the horizon of conventions-and-sentiments.

33

A GENEALOGY OF SOCIALITY

So, here is the rub, what we are imagining is that primitive human societies cultivated a symbolically augmented pathos of distance between humans and animals as practice in preparation for moments that called for the cultivation of a symbolically augmented pathos of distance between humans. To get a feeling for what we are imagining here, please recall the definition of a pathos of distance that we borrowed from Roland Barthes: "a distance that won't destroy affect [...] a distance permeated, irrigated by tender feeling: a pathos that would allow for something of Eros [affection] and Sophia [discernment]." Next, recall that a pathos of distance is what enables a society to persist when its members must be separate for a time, over the course of which they come to differ in many respects, before coming together and relating to each other again. Having recalled this, you must understand that the symbolically augmented pathos of distance that primitives cultivated between humans and animals was only ever a matter of making humans separate and unlike animals *for a time* (not for all time), and after a time humans would reconnect with and liken themselves to animals and become human-and-animal once more. In other words, the cultivation of a symbolically augmented pathos of distance between humans and animals by primitive societies generates a time during which humans make themselves differ animals in many respects but only in order to defer to animals again with respect, and, vice versa, it concomitantly yields a time during which animals differ from humans in many respects before deferring to humans again with respect.

Today, the Last Man claims that primitives are "crazy"for "seriously" believing that they can actually commune with non-human animals by way of symbols. This is because the Last Man cannot fathom the fact that the primitive is playful-and-serious about symbolic communication with animals. The Last Man believes that one is either serious or one is not, taking the difference between the two for granted, but the Last Man is both wrong and rude: it is a rude mistake to simply take the primitive seriously as opposed to playfully, and it is a rude mistake to simply take the primitive playfully as opposed to seriously. Whenever the split is made between seriousness and play by primitives, it is only made in passing, for a time (and not for all time), and the split is characterized by its time (and not for all time).

Alas, today, it seems like the only ones who still know how to treat preternatural symbolic communication with animals in a playful-and-serious, profane-and-sacred manner are young children and those artists, educators, and storytellers who respect the imaginations and the longings of young children, and who refuse to treat young children like "innocent fools".

So, many **WEiRD**-*lings today are well on their way to becoming representatives of the* **Last Man** *by the time they are teenagers, having been coddled under the roof of "innocence" during childhood only to have this roof tragically collapse around them around the time of pubescence, if they are lucky, or some time prior to pubescence, if unlucky. Following this collapse of innocence, they suffer a trauma that invites them to think in dualistic terms: with obscenity on one side and purity on the other, with sensual relations on one side and platonic relations on the other, with promiscuity on one side and abstinence on the other, with inescapable realities on one side and escapist fantasies on the other.*

For primitives, as for young children, symbolic communion with animals is, at one and the same time, playful-and-serious, an inescapable-reality-and-escapist-fantasy. Again, this is because young children and primitives recognize that they themselves are preternatural beings, at one and the same time, human-and-animal, conventional-and-sentimental, profane-and-sacred.

That being said, however, in and through the cultivation of a symbolically augmented pathos of distance between themselves and animals, primitive humans can imagine non-human and non-animal beings living above and below the horizon. On one side, above the horizon, they can imagine that there are gods: sacred supernaturals for whom life is entirely escapist fantasy. On the other side, below the horizon, they can imagine that there are beasts: profane natures for whom life is entirely an inescapable reality. What's more, in and through the cultivation of a symbolically augmented pathos of distance between humans and animals, primitives imagine that one of two things happen during times when humans differ from animals. Either humans become more like gods and animals more like beasts or, vice versa, humans become more like beasts and animals more like gods.

CHAPTER THREE

M<small>I</small><small>N</small>O<small>r</small> G<small>O</small><small>d</small><small>s</small>

So, we first imagine that the horizon is populated by preternatural beings, confusions of human-and-animal, for whom life is both inescapable-reality-and-escapist-fantasy. With the rise of the symbol on the horizon, we then imagine that there are beings above and below the horizon. Above the horizon, we imagine sacred supernaturals: gods for whom life is always an escapist fantasy. Below the horizon, we imagine profane natures: beasts for whom life is always an inescapable reality. The rise of the symbol splits the human-and-animal into the human and the animal, and stipulates that the human and the animal must tend towards opposite sides of the horizon. That being said, however, the symbol never stipulates which side either must to tend towards, allowing the human and the animal to exchange sides. What's more, the symbol both rises and sets on the horizon. When the symbol sets on the horizon, the human and the animal become the human-and-animal again, tending neither to godliness nor to beastliness but to the preternatural, to the profane-and-sacred horizon.

What we imagine, in other words, is that life within human societies is defined by rhythms composed of three differing times:

Times of beastliness, *during which humans become beastly and animals become godly, are the times during which human societies cultivate a symbolically augmented pathos of distance between humans and animals in preparation for cultivating a symbolically augmented pathos of distance between humans. Such times are defined by carnivalesque customs that express humans' grotesque bodies and repress humans' beautiful spirits. Insofar as animals do not repress their beautiful spirits, animals appear godlike relative to beast-like humans performing carnivalesque customs.*

Times of godliness, *during which humans become godly and animals become beastly, are the times during which human societies cultivate a symbolically augmented pathos of distance between humans, having prepared the way by cultivating a symbolically augmented pathos of distance between humans and animals. Such times of godliness are defined by cathartic customs that express humans' beautiful spirits and repress humans' grotesque bodies. Insofar as animals never repress their grotesque bodies, animals appear beast-like relative to god-like humans performing cathartic customs.*

Times of kindredness, *during which humans and animals defer to one another as human-and-animal, are times during which human societies do not cultivate a symbolically augmented pathos of distance, neither between humans nor between humans and animals. Such times are indefinite, without customary definition. Nothing is expressed during times of kindredness, but nor is anything repressed; rather, the singular confusion of the beautiful-spirit-and-grotesque-body is expressed-and-repressed.*

37

A GENEALOGy Of Sociality

We might characterize the rhythms of life that define human societies by resorting to metaphors drawn from agriculture. The practice of alternating times of beastliness and times of godliness is akin to the practice of rotating crops, planting one crop in preparation for another. Times of beastliness precede times of godliness in order to "fix nutrients" on the horizon for times of godliness. What's more, times of kindredness are times during which the horizon is left fallow and uncultivated so that it may renew itself and regain its fertility. Going even further, just as one might tend to the land poorly and exhaust it by never rotating crops and by never giving it time to rest and renew itself, we could say that one might also tend to the horizon poorly and exhaust the horizon by never rotating godliness and beastliness and by never allowing for fallow times, by never allowing for kindredness.

Alternatively, we might characterize the rhythms of life in human societies by resorting metaphors drawn from poetry. We might understand that times of beastliness are unaccented beats, unstressed-short syllables scansioned with an "x" and sounded with a "da". We might understand that times of godliness are accented beats, stressed-long syllables scansioned with an "/" and sounded with a "dum". What's more, we might understand that times of kindredness are pauses during which we catch our breath, silences that can be scansioned with blank spaces and unsounded. Ay, and we might claim that the rhythms of life within human societies may be varied infinitely from these three elements.

We imagine that the rhythms of life characteristic of primitive societies are defined by the relative prevalence of times of kindredness, by silences, and by the relative rarity of both times of beastliness, "da", and times of godliness, "dum". With our poetic metaphor in mind, we imagine that a rhythm of life characteristic of a primitive society could be scansioned and sounded out in the following manner x /   x x /   x x x /

DA DUM   **DA DA** DUM   **DA DA DA** DUM

Note the prevalence of blank spaces: times of kindredness prevail over all other times in this primitive rhythm. Note that times of beastliness (as indicated with "x") occur more often than times of godliness (as indicated with a "/"), but also note that times of beastliness precede and prepare for times of godliness. Note how the rarity of times of beastliness and times of godliness makes the impact of both of these times quite profound amidst the prevailing silences as you sound out this rhythm. And yet, profound though their impact may be amid silent times of kindredness, times of godliness and times of beastliness are characterized by the prevailing times of kindredness that surround them, and times of godliness and times of beastliness can be said to play a minor role in the life rhythms of primitives relative to times of kindredness. Ay, and for this is very reason, we shall call the gods that primitives imagine above the horizon "Minor Gods".

Looking ahead, we will find that "Major Gods" are imagined into being when times of godliness and times of beastliness become more prevalent and play the major role while times of kindredness become less prevalent and play the minor role. Looking even further ahead, we will find that the Absolute is imagined into being when times of kindredness recede to near oblivion, leaving only times of godliness and times of beastliness clashing against one another. Ay, and looking all the way to the finish, we will find that statistics are imagined into being when times of beastliness reign supreme and when times of godliness and times of kindredness both recede to near oblivion.

A GENEALOGY OF SOCIALITY

For the sake of comparison, let us scansion and sound out the kind of rhythm that invites us to imagine statistics into being, the kind of rhythm that defines a WEiRD life.

xxxxxxxx/xxxxxxxxxxxxxxxxxxxxx/xxxxxxxxxxxxxxxxx/xxxxxxxxxxxxxx/xxxxxxxxxxxxxxxxxxx/xxxxxxxxxxxxxx/xxxxx

DADADADADADADADADADADADADADA**DUM**DADADADA
DADADADADADADADADADADADADA
DADADADADADADADADADA**DUM**DADADADADADADADADADADADADA
DADADADADADADADADADA**DUM**DADADADADADADADADA
DADADADADADADADADADADADADA**DUM**DADADADA
DADADADADADADADADADADADADA
DADADADADADADADADADA**DUM**DADADADADADADADADADADADADA
DADADADADADADADADADA**DUM** DADADADADADADADA

Note how difficult it is to articulate this rhythm. Note how easily one loses this rhythm. Note how the times of beastliness suffocate both the times of godliness and the times of kindredness. Note how the times of kindredness are so brief and so disconnected from each other: it is very difficult to catch your breath while sounding out this rhythm. What's more, note how the rhythm drones: its times of beastliness become banal while its times of godliness and kindredness become insubstantial blips. It would take a great deal of practice, building up slowly from less droning rhythms, to manage to make the times godliness and kindredness found in this rhythm impactful.

The Last Man *is human being who has neither the motivation nor the time to practice in order to make times of godliness and kindredness impact such a beastly rhythm. The* Beyond-Human, *by contrast, is not only motivated to practice but makes time to practice in order get the better of such a beastly rhythm and to ensure that times of godliness and kindredness make an impact. Note, however, that making time to practice means finding ways to introduce times of kindredness within such a beastly rhythm or, in other words, making time to practice means stealing time (*tempo rubato*).*

CHAPTER FOUR

MAJOR GODS

The seeds that gave rise to Major Gods were planted on the horizon when humans imagined rhythms of life in which beastliness and godliness played the major roles and in which kindredness played a minor role. But these seeds didn't take root, nor sprout, nor flower, nor fruit until the humans actually realized such rhythms of life, until beastliness and godliness actually came to play the major roles and kindredness actually came to play a minor role.

As we imagine it, the rhythms of life that gave rise to Major Gods were first brought into being when humans adopted semi-sedentary foraging and horticultural life ways, but these rhythms were not fully realized until humans fully embraced agriculture and began transforming themselves into beasts of burden. The great spans of time that humans spent tending to crops on the land after embracing agriculture were beastly spans of time during which wild animals became increasingly godlike and carefree relative to human beasts of burden toiling in the fields.

The seeds that gave rise to Major Gods took root when humans transformed themselves into beasts of burden, yes, but the seeds did not sprout until humans domesticated some animals, transforming some animals into beasts of burden alongside them. Going even further, the seeds began to flower only after there emerged humans who did not labor for themselves but, instead, employed other humans and domesticated animals to labor for them. These leisured humans became more akin to wild animals in the human imagination, increasingly godlike and free spirited; meanwhile, laboring humans and domesticated animals employed in agriculture became increasingly dull and beastlike.

Finally, the seeds that give rise to Major Gods came to fruition when the duality between humans on one side and animals on the other side of the horizon was complicated by an orthogonal duality: the duality between the leisured humans and wild animals, on one side, and, on the other side, the laboring humans and domesticated animals.

43

A Genealogy of Sociality

Leisured lives are characterized by a prevalence of times of godliness relative to both times of beastliness and times of kindredness. By contrast, laboring lives are characterized by a prevalence of times of beastliness relative to times of godliness and times of kindredness. That being said, however, leisured lives are not exclusively godly and involve some beastly labors. Chief among the beastly labors of the leisured is the labor of having to issue commands: only the Major God leisures for all time, never issuing commands unless doing so at their leisure. Similarly, laboring lives are not exclusively beastly and involve some godlike leisures. Chief among the godlike leisures of the laboring is the leisure of awaiting commands: only the Monstrous Beast labors for all time, never waiting for commands unless they have been commanded to wait. What's more, leisured lives and laboring lives are not without impactful times of kindredness amidst times of godliness and beastliness, minor though these time of kindredness may be.

The emergence of the duality of leisured humans (alongside wild animals) and laboring humans (alongside domesticated animals), did not alter the symbol's stipulation that humans occupy one side of the horizon and animals the other. Rather, what the emergence of this new duality did was differentiate the *topography* of the horizon: with the leisured tending to the godly Olympian heights, to the earth's rising high into the sky; and with the laboring tending to the beastly Hadean depths, to the sky's digging deep into earth.

The primitives whom we imagined in the previous two chapters did not use the symbol to articulate the topography of the horizon: they only used the symbol to make the distinction between the earth on one side and the sky on the other side of the horizon. This is to say, in other words, that primitives didn't engage the symbol to explicate the horizon but, rather, only engaged the symbol to imply the horizon. It is only after the bifurcation of primitive into the leisured and laboring that we find the symbol explicating the horizon and differentiating heights and depths. This does not to mean that primitives had no way of differentiating leisured heights and laboring depths but, rather, it only means that they had other, non-symbolic means of differentiating the one for the other, and did not *formalize* their means of doing so by way of the symbol.

Confronted with this new duality of heights and depths, let us return to the major themes of this essay and consider this new duality with respect to these themes.

CHAPTER Four

One.

Every duality betrays a singular confusion.

Let us not assume that the duality of leisured heights and laboring depths on the horizon pre-existed the symbol's explication of the horizon. Instead, let us discover the singular confusion of the heights-and-depths, leisured-and-laboring which precedes, exceeds, and succeeds the symbol's explication of leisured heights and laboring depths.

Two

Every duality registers and remembers a mutual affinity.

The singular confusion of heights-and-depths, leisured-and-laboring is split by the symbol in order to register and remember affinities: the heights are split from the depths, the leisured from the laboring, so as to allow the sentiments of the leisured and the laboring to differ from one another for a time, not for all time, deferring back to one another again and again, time after time.

Three

It is rude to take a duality for granted, but one can make amends for one's rudeness by acknowledging the singular confusion that precedes, exceeds, and succeeds a duality.

It is rude to take for granted the split between the heights and the depths, leisured and the laboring, just as it is rude to take the split between humans and animals for granted. Upon encountering such rudeness, the leisured and the laboring will protest, "How rudely you assume a difference between us? Do not take us for granted. Rightly, we do make ourselves different for a time, but we can only make ourselves different via the splitting of the singular confusion of heights-and-depths, leisure-and-labor, on the horizon. What's more the differences between us fade and blur over time and it have to be remade time and time again if they are to be re-used again and again."

A GENEALOGY OF SOCIALITY

We WEiRD-lings tend to be rude: we tend to take dualities for granted and to argue whether these dualities are to be regarded as extremes on a continuum, or turns of a cycle, or exclusive dichotomies. Inasmuch as we tend to assume dualities, we WEiRD-lings tend to deny or ignore the precession, excession, and succession of singular confusions: the human-and-animal, the conventional-and-sentimental, the profane-and-sacred, the heights-and-depths, the leisured-and-laboring. More remarkably still, we WEiRD-lings tend to assume that people living in primitive and prehistoric societies are either as rude as we are or even ruder, which is to say, in other words, that we WEiRD-lings project our dualisms onto primitive and prehistoric societies, and we assume that primitive and prehistoric societies take as much for granted as we do, if not more.

We must remark upon these tendencies of WEiRD-lings because, thus far in our Genealogy, we have only dealt with primitive and prehistoric societies. Humans imagined Major Gods into being, like the Olympians and the Titans, long before they ever imagined proper historical records into being. Indeed, by the time humans imagined historical records into being, the seeds of the Absolute had been sown on the horizon, for one cannot imagine historical records into being without also imagining the existence of the Absolute.

The Absolute is imagined into being when times of kindredness recede to near oblivion, leaving only times of godliness and times of beastliness clashing against one another. Major Gods are imagined into being when times of godliness and times of beastliness become increasingly prevalent, yes, but times of kindredness though less prevalent, continue to play a minor role in the imagining of Major Gods. When times of kindredness play even a minor role in the life rhythms of human societies, humans must have some regard and respect for indefinite times, for times without customary definitions. Having regard and respect for indefinite times, no matter how minor, makes it difficult to imagine such a thing as an "accurate" historical record of any kind. Indeed, one can only begin to imagine "accurate" historical records when one can imagine times of kindredness receding into oblivion and all time becoming customarily defined, becoming either godly or beastly.

CHAPTER FOUR

We first imagine the Absolute and "accurate" historical records into being when times of kindredness become so minimal that they can only be regarded in one of two ways: (i) by looking forwards into the distant future and backwards into the distant past in a telescopic manner, or (ii) by looking at the present in microscopic manner. Ay, and it is only after imagining the Absolute and "accurate" historical records into being that humans begin to reject singular confusions and to take dualities for granted, regarding everything in logical terms, as either continuous, circuitous, or dichotomous. It is in the next chapter, in which we imagine the Absolute into existence, that our WEiRD rudenesses will begin to have some purchase. And yet, even in the next chapter, we will need to be wary of taking such rudeness for granted.

CHAPTER FIVE

THE ABSOLUTE

In chapter three, we found that Minor Gods were imagined into being when the symbol differentiated the horizon, splitting the earth from the sky. In chapter four, we found that Major Gods were imagined into being when the symbol differentiated the topography of the horizon, splitting heights from depths. In this chapter, the fifth, we will find the Absolute imagined into being when the symbol differentiates our scope of vision on the horizon, differentiating telescopic vision from microscopic vision.

The Absolute is a figure so telescopic that it makes everything near and dear to earth appear microscopic. The emergence of the figure the Absolute marks the first coming of the Last Man, he who threatens the horizon by proposing that the sky ought to swallow the earth, he for whom the symbol never sets on the horizon. If today we WEiRD-lings are nostalgic for rhythms of life that yielded the Absolute, this is only because the Absolute invites us to dispense with microscopic details and to regard the vast scheme of things. We WEiRD-lings are desperate to dispense with microscopic details because we live in the wake of the second coming of the Last Man, the one who has ditched the Absolute for statistics. The rhythms of our WEiRD lives, the rhythms that yield (to) statistics, drown us in increasingly microscopic details, leaving us with no time to consider the vast scheme of things.

The Absolute emerges within human societies that have become so large and complex that the perspective of the laboring becomes increasingly microscopic and the perspective of the leisured becomes increasingly telescopic. What the Agricultural Revolution achieved for Major Gods, the Urban Revolution achieves for the Absolute. The seeds of the Absolute first took root during the First Wave of the Urban Revolution, during the process by which small, kin-based, non-literate agricultural villages were transformed into large, socially complex, literate urban societies. But the Absolute only sprouted and flowered with later waves of the urban revolution, as immense cities became the capitals of cosmopolitan world empires. It was the rise of empires that transformed laboring into an unceasing drone of beastliness, utterly lacking in godliness and kindredness, making laboring perspectives "all too microscopic". Concomitantly, the rise of empires transformed the lives of the leisured into an unceasing drone of godliness, lacking in beastliness and kindredness, making leisured perspectives "all too telescopic".

49

A GENEALOGY OF SOCIALITY

Both the leisured and the laboring lost out with the urban revolution and the rise of empires, and what they both lost, above all else, were times of kindredness. Craving kindredness but lacking it, the leisured, from their increasingly exalted perspectives, began to telescopically attend to the ample times of kindredness to be found in the distant past-and-future, before-life-and-after-death. Meanwhile, the laboring, also craving kindredness but lacking it, had to attend to the microscopic times of kindredness from their increasingly lowly perspectives, to matters of life-and-death in the here-and-now.

Please, if you will, indulge us a Cartesian geometric metaphor. Having already regarded the X-axis that splits earth-and-sky and the Y-axis that splits heights-and-depths, we are now dealing with the Z-axis that splits near-from-far. On the highest mountains one can attend to what is far, but within the deepest caverns one can only attend to what is near. The telescope allows the exalted on the mountaintop to tend to what is furthest from them; the microscope allows the lowly in the deepest pit to tend to what is nearest to them. The more precipitously high you get, the more and more you will tend to regard matters telescopically. The more abysmally low you get, the more and more you will tend to regard matters microscopically. With the urban revolution and the rise of empire, the heights of leisure became precipitous and the depths of labor became abysmal, and this effectively split the nearsighted and the farsighted, the microscopic and the telescopic. Those laboring in the abysses became more and more microscopic and nearsighted, while those leisuring on the peaks tended more and more to the telescopic and farsighted.

Ay, and so we have a new duality here: the duality of the near and the far, the microscopic and the telescopic. With this new duality in mind, let us return to the themes of this essay once more.

CHAPTER FIVE

ONE.

Every duality betrays a singular confusion.

Let us not assume the pre-existence of the duality of near and far, microscopic and telescopic. Instead, let us discover the singular confusion of the near-and-far, microscopic-and-telescopic, which precedes, exceeds, and succeeds the symbol's explication of near and far, microscopic and telescopic.

Two

Every duality registers and remembers a mutual affinity.

The singular confusion of the near-and-far, microscopic-and-telescopic, is split by the symbol in order to register and remember affinities: the near is split from the far, the microscopic from the telescopic, so as to allow the sentiments of the nearsighted and the farsighted to differ from one another for a time, but not for all time, deferring back to one another again and again, time after time.

Three

It is rude to take a duality for granted, but one can make amends for one's rudeness by acknowledging the singular confusion that precedes, exceeds, and succeeds a duality.

It is rude to take it for granted the split between the near and the far, between the microscopic and the telescopic, just as it is rude to take the a split between humans and animals for granted, and it is rude to take the split between leisure and labor for granted. Ay, but here's the rub: once the symbol is operative on three different dimensions, rudeness becomes unavoidable, and hard to protest against. Here we are finally at the point in our story where rudeness can be taken for granted. For the symbol renders societies in two dimensions: just like a three dimensional spatial form represented on a two dimensional plane is a rude approximation, a three dimensional society rendered in two dimensions by the symbol is a rude approximation.

51

A Genealogy of Sociality

With rudeness having become unavoidable and a source of social strife, it happens that, rather than admitting that those treated rudely are victims of circumstance treated undeservedly, humans began come up with *reasons* to believe that those on the receiving end of rudenesses deserved to be treated rudely. Indeed, the laboring began to rudely reason that the leisured are leisured because they are "naturally" oblivious to what is near to them when, in fact, prolonged leisure is what makes the leisured oblivious to what is near. Vice versa, the leisured began to rudely reason that the laboring are laboring because they are "naturally" oblivious to what is far from them when, in fact, prolonged labor is what makes the laboring oblivious to what is far.

We imagine that this rude reasoning on both sides lead to resentments and that the figure of the Absolute emerged a means to level resentments. On the one side, those laboring in the abysses turned to the figure of the Absolute in order to claim level footing with those leisuring on the peaks and to claim the right to judge the behavior of the leisured according to their own nearsighted measures. On the other side, those leisuring on the peaks turned to the figure of the Absolute in order to deny having higher responsibilities and to claim that they should not be judged according to more farsighted measures. Indeed, we imagine that the Absolute first emerged as a means for the laboring to lower the leisured back down to earth and to hold the leisured responsible, but, subsequently, the leisured, having been lowered, turned the Absolute against the laboring and employed the Absolute as a means to deny any and all higher responsibilities. Regardless of whether the Absolute was used to hold others responsible or to elude responsibility, the Absolute achieved the same thing: the distance between those leisuring on peaks and those laboring in abysses was diminished and became microscopic relative to the Absolute's vast scheme of things. In sum, with the figure of the Absolute, for the first time ever, the symbol was not used to enable a pathos to traverse significant distances but, rather, it was used to render distances insignificant.

From the perspective of the Absolute, the earth becomes a mere point in the vastness of the sky and, as such, the horizon of earth-and-sky becomes naught but an infinitesimal halo around a point in the vastness. Indeed, from the astronomical perspective of the all encompassing Absolute, all beings near and dear to the earth, including wild animals and domesticated animals, leisured humans and laboringhumans, are beings approaching one and the same profane nature. This is evidenced by the fact that, whereas the whims of wild animals and the vagaries of the elements are the models for the irrational whims of Major Gods, the fixed geometric movements of the planets and stars are the model for the rational will of the all encompassing Absolute. Whereas times of godliness with respect to Major Gods were times at which one felt like a free spirit, living according to one's whims; times of godliness with respect to the Absolute are times in which one finds oneself following a fixed and rational course of action. The pivot between these two different modes of godliness, between the whimsical godliness Major Gods and the rational godliness Absolute, is most suggestive. During this pivot, Major Gods became increasingly telescopic and were associated less with the whims of wild animals and the vagaries of the elements and more with the "wandering stars" navigating the "fixed stars". After this pivot, the Absolute emerged as being (or nothingness) modeled on the vast expanse that encompasses all of the fixed stars in their motionless relations to one another as well as the wandering stars.

Insofar as life is full of accidents, fortuitous and surprising happenings, and wandering motions, life is, for the most part and for most people, full of times of beastliness relative to the Absolute. Only the idealist, who aims to transform their life into a set of fixed routines, who is able to rid their life of wandering motions, can be said to have a life that is close to godliness relative to the Absolute. Indeed, relative to the Absolute, it is not the distinction between the leisured and laboring that matters but, rather, what matters is the distinction between the godliness of ideal ways of life, on the one side, and, on the other side, the beastliness of materialistic ways of life.

Going further, the idealist is to be regarded as the first "human, all too human" figure, the first coming of the Last Man. *Recall that the main social distinction with respect to Minor Gods was the distinction between human and animal, with neither one being exclusively godly or beastly but, rather, with the two taking turns on opposite sides: humans becoming godly and animals beastly then, vice versa, animals becoming godly and humans beastly. Recall that operative social distinction with respect to Major Gods was the distinction between the godly leisured life and the beastly laboring life, with leisured humans and wild animals being godly, and with laboring humans and domesticated animals being beastly. What you will notice is that both humans and animals could become godly with respect to Minor Gods and Major Gods. By contrast, no animal becomes godly with respect to the Absolute because no animal ever becomes an idealist: no animal comes close to ridding life of accidents and wandering motions. Indeed, it can be taken for granted that all animals are beastly with respect to (and for) the Absolute, and what's more it can also be taken for granted that most humans are beastly too.*

And yet, although the earth is but a speck for the Absolute, and although everything on earth tends to profanity and beastliness, the earth has the advantage of being the speck *at the center* of the vast scheme of things. Heights-and-depths, nearer-and-further on the horizon might be rendered infinitesimal by the Absolute, but they remain of a paramount significance, for they are at the center of the Absolute's scheme. Heights-and-depths, nearer-and-further on the horizon become infinitesimal differences that mean almost nothing on their own but that can mean a great when regarded as integral to formations on the horizon upon which the vast scheme of things turns. Thus, although the Absolute diminishes the horizon to an infinitesimal halo surrounding a point, the Absolute cannot entirely obliterate the horizon.

Thus, relative to the Absolute, the horizon is to be re-discovered in and through the descent to the infinitesimal. Or, in other words, we may discover the horizon and its heights and depths by imagining that the universe turns on "clinamina"*, on unpredictable swerves of infinitesimal magnitudes that occur "at no fixed place or time", lacking extension but having intense significance. Ascents to Olympian heights and descents to Hadean depths, which had been experienced as extensive-and-intensive journeys with regard to Major Gods, are now only experienced as intensive journeys with regard to the Absolute.*

So, on one side, there is the "human, all too human" figure of the idealist, the figure who lives according to fixed routines that are extensions of the logic of the Absolute. But on the other side, there is also the human-and-animal figure of the materialist, the figure whose weyward wandering are intensifications of the will of the Absolute. Refusing to take the duality between the materialist and the idealist for granted, we invite you to imagine a figure who is idealistic-and-materialistic, a figure whose singularly confused lifestyle, simultaneously wandering-and-fixed, is an intensification-and-extension of the will of the Absolute. This is the original figure of the Beyond-Human *who regards the horizon with increasing respect in spite of the Absolute.*

CHAPTER SIX

Turning and turning in the widening gyre
The falcon cannot hear the falconer;
Things fall apart; the centre cannot hold;
Mere anarchy is loosed upon the world,
The blood-dimmed tide is loosed, and everywhere
The ceremony of innocence is drowned;
The best lack all conviction, while the worst
Are full of passionate intensity.

— William Butler Yeats *from* The Second Coming

StatiStiCS

The Absolute was the figure that characterized the first coming of the Last Man. *Statistics are the figures that characterize the second coming of the* Last Man. *At the end of the last chapter, it seemed as if the horizon had outmaneuvered and outwitted the symbol in and through its descent to the infinitesimal, enabling the* Beyond–Human *to overcome the* Last Man. *Alas, the* Last Man *now returns with a vengeance to wage war on infinitesimals by means of statistics.*

Every infinitesimal is a differential that is integral to local-and-global formations on the horizon, to heights-and-depths, nearer-and-further on the horizon. Every statistic, by contrast, is a bit of information, a datum, generated by disintegrating formations on the horizon, by smashing heights-and-depths, nearer-and-further on the horizon into discrete particles. In other words, statistics are the end result of atomizations that obliterate formations on the horizon and, coterminously, obliterate forms of sociality.

The Industrial Revolution did for statistics, what the Agricultural Revolution did for Major Gods and the Urban Revolution did for the Absolute. Ay, and just like the Agricultural Revolution and the Urban Revolution, the Industrial Revolution came in waves. Statistics first took root with the First Wave of the Industrial Revolution: with the mechanization of production being spurred along by the emergence of population statistics, the atomization of populations into discrete "peoples" (e.g., ethnicities, nations, races). Statistics sprouted with the Second Wave Industrial Revolution: with the electrification of production being spurred along by the decomposition of population statistics into individual statistics, the atomization of "peoples" into discrete "persons". Statistics is now flowering with the Third Wave of Industrial Revolution: with the digitization of production being spurred along by the decomposition of individual statistics into dividual statistics, the atomization of individual persons into discrete "dispositions".

Though we recognize the important role that the different waves of the Industrial Revolution played in the development of statistics, we will focus here on the Copernican Revolution, which will reveals far more about the rise of statistics in our imagination.

A GENEALOGy Of SOCIALITY

With the Copernican Revolution, the earth, which had been at the center of the Absolute's vast scheme of things, became just another speck at the margins of a vast universe. Before the Copernican Revolution, everything in the sky turned on the earth, everything's turning depended upon the infinitesimal horizon that related the earth and sky. After the Copernican Revolution, the earth and its solar system become just another far flung region in a vastness, and we find that we can no longer easily relate the earth and its solar system to the cosmos as a whole. That being said, however, we can now more easily relate the earth and its solar system to other far flung regions of the vastness by treating the region that containing the earth and its solar system as a statistical aggregate and treating the earth as a [in]dividual statistic within that aggregate.

The infinitesimal heights-and-depths, nearer-and-further on the earth have, thus, become insignificant, and what matters are the statistical aggregates of heights and depths, nearer and further: the mean, the median, the mode, and the standard deviation of the earth's heights and earth's depths. What's more, the vast expanse is no longer important in and of itself but the different regions of the expanse are. The importance of the different regions is found in their being subjected to statistical analysis relative to our own region, as we scour the vast expanse for earth-like planets. Indeed, just as we say that many people can't see the forest for all the trees that populate it, we might say that many people can no longer see the sky for all the probable earths and solar systems that populate it. Ay, and this is what we mean when we say that the earth now threatens to suffocate the sky.

To become subject to statistical analysis is to become beastly. Statistics about elephant populations living on a given region of the earth do not deal with elephants as social animals, as preternatural beings that can inspire social sentiments in us. Rather, such statistics deal with elephants as beasts of a calculably profane nature that occupy a given region of the planet that is statistically more or less like others. Is it any wonder that statistics on elephant population losses do not spur social sentiments in us while social sentiments are triggered when we hear a story about how one singular herd of elephants is traumatized by the poaching of their matriarch? Statistics only inspire us to regard elephants in beastly ways and to use beastly phrases (e.g., "low fertility rates") that do not acknowledge the elephants' sentiments.

Within human societies, today's identity politics are a beastly politics of statistical identities. I am counted as black, counted as a man, counted as underemployed, and I am told that what I am counted as ought to determine my interests. What's more, above all else, I am told to fear not being counted for something, not making myself count, and counting for less than I should.

Doing otherwise than I am told, however, I wonder why I should make myself countable if my being counted isn't inspired or inspiring? What's more, I also wonder whether I can inspire or be inspired without making myself count?

In our age, the age of the WEIRD-ness, to become a statistician, and to subject others to statistical analysis, is to become godly. During the First and Second Waves of the Industrial Revolution, the human bureaucrat who analyzed statistics was the godlike figure. Since the Third Wave of the Industrial Revolution, however, it is the man-made automated machine, the computer running an algorithm, that more and more subjects the world to statistical analysis: humans are becoming more and more beastly, while computing machines are becoming more and more godlike.

When one does not count, is not counted, or is under-counted, one does not properly figure in the analyses of algorithms, executed by man or machine, and this is akin to being forsaken the gods. To be favored by the gods is to make everything about you count and count highly. The Last Man of the second coming is always counting: counting his calories, counting his steps, counting his sleeping hours, counting his friends and followers, counting his credits and debits, counting his carbon footprint. The Last Man feeds these counts to algorithms and it feels to him like sacrificing his own beastly flesh to a god. These algorithms process the Last Man's stats and give him his percentile rank relative to others, and they advise the Last Man on how he might optimize his stats and increase his percentile rank. Today's liberal is the smug Last Man who wants algorithms to help him "level the playing field" so as to rank peoples, persons, dispositions "fairly and objectively". Today's illiberal reactionary is the aggrieved Last Man who wants algorithms to help him "incline the playing field" in his favor, so that his people, his person, and his dispositions gain rank over other peoples, other persons, and other dispositions.

A GENEALOGy Of SOCIALITY

The Last Man, *working to maximize his percentile rank, believes that it is best to rise to a high rank early in life and to plateau at a sustainable height for the rest of one's life. It is not helpful summit and then descend Olympian peaks, and it is detrimental to plunge down into and climb up out of Hadean pits. From the perspective of an algorithm, a dynamic life — a life characterized by great heights, great depths, and fortuitous turns — is a life of middling rank. In our* WEiRD *societies, those who consistently score in the 99th percentile, in the top 1%, are those who rule but they are also those whose lives lack dynamism, those who will never learn how to weather dramatic fortuitous ups and downs with grace. Indeed, it is no wonder that* WEiRD *societies are societies ruled without dynamism and grace...*

Recall again that the main social distinction with respect to Minor Gods was the distinction between human and animal, with neither one being exclusively godly or beastly but, rather, with the two taking turns becoming godly and becoming beastly: humans becoming godly and animals beastly then, vice versa, animals becoming godly and humans beastly. Recall next that the operative social distinction with respect to Major Gods was the distinction between godly leisure and beastly labor, with the human-and-animal on both sides: leisured humans and wild animals being godly and laboring humans and domesticated animals being beastly. Next, recall that the operative social distinction with respect to the Absolute was the distinction between the godly idealist's life of fixed routines, which was exclusively human, and the beastly materialist's life of weyward wanderings, which was human-and-animal. With statistics there emerges a new social distinction: the distinction between (i) the godly statistician, the human or human-made machine, subjecting the world statistical analysis, and (ii) the beastly noise, human-and-animal, that corrupts, distorts, and impedes statistical analysis.

The figure of the statistician, no matter whether human or human-made machine, is a "human, all too human" figure, just like the figure of the idealist. Just as no animals become idealists, no animals become statisticians. The tie that binds the idealist and the statistician is their humanity, their being human first, foremost, and above all else. That being said, however, the idealist finds that the animal has to be regarded with respect and deferred to in many respects because the Absolute's vast scheme of things turns on the infinitesimal human-and-animal horizon. The statistician, unlike the idealist, believes that the animal that makes a beastly noise, that cannot or will not be properly counted, is an expendable animal, a worthless thing.

We introduced this essay with a quote from Aristotle's **Politics**:

Man is by nature a social animal; an individual who is unsocial naturally and not accidentally is either beneath our notice or more than human. Society is something that precedes the individual. Anyone who either cannot lead the common life or is so self-sufficient as not to need to, and therefore does not partake of society, is either a beast or a god.

The **Last Man** of the second coming, reflecting upon Aristotle's claim, protests, "There is no such a thing as society. There are only beastly individuals and godlike algorithms. Man is by nature that beastly individual that engineers and serves godlike algorithms. So, quite naturally, Man is ranked first among beasts, and those who engineer and serve the most all-consuming algorithms are ranked first amongst Man. Non-human beasts, those who do not engineer and serve algorithms themselves, may be counted by Man, yes, but only as second to Man, and they may only serve algorithms indirectly through Man. The non-human beast that Man is either unable or unwilling to count is an expendable beast, to be excluded from our calculations and exterminated from existence."

A Genealogy of Sociality

The first to assume the logic of the Last Man in this regard were the Western bureaucrats and soldiers who oversaw genocides and slavery as part of the Colonization of the Americas, famines in Asia as part of the Late Victorian Holocausts, the Rape of Africa as part of the New Imperialism, and the many other atrocities that Western Man perpetrated on the rest of humankind preceding and following the First Wave of the Industrial Revolution. Godly algorithms became beastly flesh as Western Man became Last Man on a mission to exclude and exterminate all the expendable brutes of the non-Western world. Subsequently, between the Second and Third Waves of the Industrial Revolution, Western Man as Last Man turned on himself, seeking to exclude and exterminate the expendable brute within via "Wars to End All Wars", "Final Solutions", and "Weapons of Mass Destruction".

These "triumphs" aside, however, the logic of the Last Man has only recently revealed itself in earnest, in our own time, with the culmination of the Third Wave of the Industrial Revolution, with Big Data, A.I., and other "Weapons of Math Destruction". Today, godly algorithms have transcended beastly flesh and become machines. These machines, like Deep Blue, Watson, and AlphaGo, analyze statistics so as to out perform the Last Man at games of logic and fact finding. With machines having proven themselves more capable of subjecting matters to statistical analysis than any human being, it can now be taken for granted that all animals are beastly, including the human. Only machines, the children of humanity, are properly godly. With this final "triumph", the Last Man composes his "happy ending" for all of history, "Counted first amongst beasts by his darling children, by his machines, Man lived happily ever after to the end of his days, all watched over by machines of loving grace."

For those of us, human-and-animal, who are neither counted amongst nor counted by the Last Man and his machines, this "happy ending" is the nightmare scenario of our final exclusion and extermination by machines. Thankfully, however, this "happy" ending is not a foregone conclusion. The horizon is being obliterated by statistics, surely, but the horizon haunts its obliterator in and through its being obliterated. There is still such a thing as society in spite of the "triumph" of statistics: society persists and insists as a ghostly thing, but it persists and insists nonetheless, spectral though it may be.

In brief, society persists and insists, in spite of statistics, as spectra of possibilities haunting statistics. Spectra of possible populations haunt each and every population statistic; spectra of possible individuals haunt each and every individual statistic; and spectra of possible dividuals haunt each and every dividual statistic. Take, for instance, the statistic that the average person in the United States has seven sexual partners in a lifetime. This statistic is haunted by vast spectra of different possible sexual relationships — imagined-and-real relationships, consummated-and-unconsummated relationships, consensual-and-non-consensual relationships, pleasurable-and-painful relationships—and no statistical analysis, no matter how granular, could ever accurately figure this spectra out. We can rediscover society by endeavoring to attune ourselves to the spectra of possibilities haunting statistics, by characterizing and contextualizing statistics in possible way that we can conceive of.

In the Age of the Absolute we found that the descent to the infinitesimal re-discovered the horizon when the Absolute threatened to obliterate the horizon by marshaling the sky to swallow the earth. In the Age of Statistics we find that attunement to the spectral re-discovers the horizon when statistics threaten to obliterate the horizon by marshaling the earth to suffocate the sky. Today, every time we regard the vast expanse with a statistical eye, searching for statistical likenesses of our earth and solar system, we ought to recognize that every statistical likeness we discover is haunted by spectra of possibilities, and we may regard and respect the vast expanse as a field suffused with so many spectral horizons.

Thus, on one side, we have the figure of the godly statistician, the one *who subjects others to statistical analysis. On the other side, we have the figure of beastly noise, the spectral* other *that haunts statistical analyses. Not taking the duality between godly statistician and beastly noise for granted, we invite you to imagine a statistical-and-spectral figure, a figure who is simultaneously statistician-and-noise, a being who knows themself and is known by others in and through the singular confusion of analysis-and-attunement. This figure is the figure of the* Beyond-Human *who regards the horizon with ever increasing respect in spite of statistics.*

63

IN LIEU OF A CONCLUSION

[OBERST ENZIAN:] *"Well, I think we're here, but only in a statistical way. Something like that rock over there is just about 100% certain—it knows it's there, so does everybody else. But our own chances of being right here right now are only a little better than even—the slightest shift in the probabilities and we're gone—schnapp! like That."*

[INTERLOCUTOR:] *"Peculiar talk, Oberst."*

[ENZIAN:] *"Not if you've been where we have. Forty years ago, in Südwest, we were nearly exterminated. There was no reason. Can you understand that? No reason. We couldn't even find comfort in the Will of God Theory. These were Germans with names and service records, men in blue uniforms who killed clumsily and not without guilt. Search-and-destroy missions, every day. It went on for two years. The orders came down from a human being, a scrupulous butcher named von Trotha. The thumb of mercy never touched his scales.*

"We have a word that we whisper, a mantra for times that threaten to be bad. Mba-kayere. You may find that it will work for you. Mba-kayere. It means 'I am passed over.' *To those of us who survived von Trotha, it also means that we have learned to stand outside our history and watch it, without feeling too much. A little schizoid. A sense for the statistics of our being.*

—Thomas Pynchon *from* Gravity's Rainbow

InterErlude:

On

Trans_formation

(Beyond In_formation}

ONe.

A coyote passes over your backyard on a rainy day, leaving a footprint
in a patch of dirt in your garden.
The coyote's "act of passing over",
which leaves the footprint in the patch of dirt,
is the "trans-formation" of a substrate.
The footprint left behind in the dirt
is the "residue" of the coyote's act of passing over:
it is the "in-formation" of the trans-formation.

Two.

"Trans-formations" or "acts of passing over"
precede, exceed and succeed
"in-formations" or "residues of passing over".
Returning to our example above,
the coyote's act of passing over your yard
began before it left its footprint,
happened as it left its footprint,
and carried on after it left its footprint.

THRee.

Logical analysis, as in-formation processing,
involves retrospections on past trans-formations
and prospections on future trans-formations,
but does not involve "on-going trans-formations".
Of course, in-formation processing is itself an "on-going trans-formation",
but in-formation processing does not "involve" itself,
it does not "turn on itself" as an on-going trans-formation.
Rather than turning on itself as a trans-formation, in-formation processing
turns on and evolves from in-formation.
In other words, in-formation processing is an "act of passing over"
that turns on and evolves from "residues of passing over".

FᴼᴜR.

Beyond logical analysis as information processing,
 I would like to consider sentimental attunement
  as trans-formation processing.
Sentimental attunement is self-situating and self-motivating information processing;
 it is an ongoing trans-formation that "involves" and "turns on" itself
  as an "act of passing over".
Returning to the anecdote of the coyote's act of passing over one's yard,
 the sentiment that one experiences upon seeing
  a coyote's footprint in the dirt
   goes beyond one's processing of the in-formation
    that a coyote has passed over and
     may (or may not) return.
Briefly put, the sentiment precedes, exceeds, and succeeds
 all retrospection and prospection by adding a situation and a motivation
  (real or imagined) to the mix.
One imagines the circumstances under which one might hunt the coyote
 and one experiences one sentiment.
One imagines the circumstances under which one might be hunted by the coyote a
 and one experiences a second sentiment.
One recalls the circumstances under which one last encountered a coyote
 and one experiences a third sentiment.
One imagines oneself as a hungry coyote searching for food
 and one experiences a fourth sentiment.
Considering all four of the aforementioned circumstances simultaneously,
 one experiences a fifth sentiment
  that "confuses" or "superposes" four different sentiments.
To be attuned to one's sentiments is to be able to express
 the different sentiments evoked when situating and motivating
  a given bit of information,
   both as distinct sentimental dispositions
    and as the confused constituents
     of a sentimental superposition.

ƒIVE.

If one wants to attend to on-going transformations, one must to attend to problems
enabling sentimental attunement, going beyond any and all problems
enabling logical analysis.
Otherwise, if one only attends to problems enabling logical analysis,
one will always be dealing with trans-formations
in retrospect and as prospects.

sIX.

Take the problem of climate change.
We attend to the problem of climate change as if it is only a problem enabling
logical analysis when we only attend to the effects
of our carbon footprints without attending to how we affect
and are affected by our carbon footprints.
This is to say, in other words, that we keep ourselves
from affecting and being affected by on-going trans-formations
of the earth's climate when we attend to climate change
as if it is only a problem enabling logical analysis.
Climate change must be regarded as a problem enabling sentimental attunement,
as a problem beyond logical analysis,
if we are to affect and be affected by on-going trans-formations
of the earth's climate.
We must go beyond knowing causes in retrospect and knowing our prospects,
and we must situate ourselves and motivate ourselves to engage
with climate change as an on-going process.
The dissemination of scientific facts and figures regarding emissions will,
on its own, only reify both past mistakes and future disasters.
To act upon on-going trans-formations of the earth's climate,
we need science fictions and fabulations to attune us
to on-going trans-formations of the earth's climate.

SEVEN.

Science, broadly speaking, in-forms life.
Art, broadly speaking, trans-forms life.
Science enables in-formation processing:
      it revolves around problems enabling logical analyses,
          and it treats matters in retrospect and as prospects.
Art enables trans-formation processing:
      it revolves around problems enabling sentimental attunement,
          and it treats on-going matters by situating us and motivating us
             to think, to feel, and to do in an on-going manner.
A culture that invests more in science than it does in art
      is a culture that generates a preponderance of in-formation
          in order to resolve itself against trans-formations.
That being said, however, art is most trans-formative
      when it is suffused with science.
Meaning that a culture that invests in art
      but excludes science from the arts
          is only another kind of culture that resolves itself
             against trans-formations.

EIGHT.

Philosophy, as I conceive of it and as I would practice it,
      is the practice of joining art with science
          so as to augment art's capacity to trans-form life
             and science's capacity to in-form life.
Every philosophy is an act of passage from in-formation processing
      to trans-formation processing and back again,
          an act that joins together problems enabling logical analysis
             and problems enabling sentimental attunement
                so as to create problems enabling
                   analysis-and-attunement.
A culture that does not invest in philosophy
      alongside science and art
          is yet another kind of culture that
             resolves itself against trans-formations.

NINE.

One cannot trans-form one's own life in a radical way unless
one can find ways and means of doing science-and-philosophy-and-art.
What's more, one cannot enable others to trans-form their own lives in radical ways
unless one can help others find ways and means
of doing science-and-philosophy-and-art.
It follows that there are cultures that resolve themselves against trans-formations
by making science, philosophy, and art the preserves
of an "aristocracy" or "meritocracy": a class of "achievers"
who would protect their cultures against
radical trans-formations so long as
their cultures recognize and honor
their "achievements".

TEN.

A counterculture is a culture that catalyzes radical trans-formations
by refusing to reserve science, philosophy, and art for "achievers",
and by making science-and-philosophy-and-art accessible to
"attempters".

Land Other, Child and (M)other

Featuring appendages and organs scavenged from the corpi of psychoanalysis, schizoanalysis, and deconstruction, the concepts included in the Frankensteinish compendium that follows were selected and developed in order to assist readers in their own personal search for an answer to the question, "How do I relate to others?"

The germ from which these concepts have developed is the proposition that the mother is the prototype of the other, and that one's relationship with one's mother is prototypical with respect to all one's relationships with others. That being said, I am NOT proposing that one's relationship with one's mother is representative of all one's relationships with others. To the contrary, as I understand it, the prototype of a given product is not representative of the product but, rather, it is suggestive of it. Following from this, I am proposing that one's relationship with one's mother is only suggestive of all one's relationships with others.

A person might suggest to you that you do something foolish, like stick your tongue in an electric socket, but it is up to you to take the suggestion or leave it. Similarly, while your relationship with your mother suggests ways of relating to others, it is up to you to take these suggestions or leave them. That being said, however, the "power of suggestion" must be reckoned with. If you scoff at the suggestion that you should put your tongue in an electric socket, this is only because this suggestion has little power over you. There are, no doubt, some foolish suggestions that have had and will have a greater power over you. It follows from this that one's relationship with one's mother can be more or less suggestive, can have a greater or lesser power of suggestion.

Thinking this matter through a little further, one's relationship with one's mother is not the only suggestive relationship that one might have with others. Indeed, it is very possible that one might have a relationship with another person that is more suggestive, that has a greater power of suggestion than one's relationship with one's mother. The more suggestive a relationship is, the more prototypical the relationship, and, insofar as there are relationships with others that are more suggestive than one's relationship with one's mother, there can be relationships with others that are more prototypical than one's relationship with one's mother. In this text, we will use the neologism "(m)other" to refer to any and every other with whom one has a suggestive, prototypical relationship, including but not limited to one's mother(s).

73

A relationship becomes suggestive for an individual when a relationship eases an individual's anxieties, and others become (m)others to an individual when an individual relates to others in order to ease their anxieties. There are no limits to the others that can become (m)others, as an individual may seek to ease their anxieties by relating to others of all kinds: human-and-nonhuman, animate-and-inanimate, singular-and-plural. Ay, and insofar there are others who have related themselves to you in order to ease their anxieties, you have become (m)other to others, whether or not you can or have mothered a child in the conventional sense.

The greater the anxieties eased by the (m)other in a relationship, the more suggestive the relationship becomes and the more prototypical the (m)other becomes. The lesser the anxieties eased by the (m)other in a relationship, the less suggestive the relationship becomes and the less prototypical the (m)other becomes. Is there any greater anxiety than that of being born? If not, then there cannot be a more suggestive relationship than one's relationship with one's mother, she who eased the anxieties that attended one's birth. Some say, however, that the greatest anxiety in life isn't the anxiety of being born but, rather, the anxiety about and around death and dying. If they are right, then one's most suggestive relationships will be one's relationships with (m)others who ease one's anxiety about and around death and dying. Then again, there are still others who say that there are anxieties between birth-and-death that are greater than both the anxieties that attend birth and the anxieties about and around death and dying. If so, then it may be that the most suggestive relationship in one's life will be with the (m)others who ease an anxiety arising amidst birth-and-death but other than that of birth or death.

Regardless of which relation is the most suggestive, the most prototypical, the most (m)otherly, it is the relation between child and mother is the relation most likely to be shared widely amongst the readers of this text. For this reason, and for this reason only, I have cast the child-mother relation as the archetypal relation at the origin, the zero point for the set of conceptual coordinates that I have provided here, the fixed point of reference for my geometry of relations with others. Then again, insofar as relations with others precede, exceed, and succeed all metrics and are beyond all measure, it might be more accurate to say that I have cast the child-mother relation as the base-point for my topology of relations with others

One last note before beginning, please understand that the concepts included in this compendium do not themselves ask and answer the question, "How do I relate to others?" The concepts below only suggest some different ways of asking and answering the question. I invite you to take these suggestions or leave them.

As you will...

THE NARRATIVE Of UR_CREATION.

ThE BEYOND BEfOrE ThEPLEASUrEPRINCIPLE.

[The story of how you have been pleased by a [m]other.]

The baby feels hunger (an increase of anxiety); the baby cries (an spontaneous reaction to increasing anxiety); a (m)other attends to the baby's cries, giving the baby milk from her breast (an anxiety relieving encounter with a (m)other); the baby's hunger subsides (a decrease of anxiety).

The result: the un-conscious arche-writing of a memory and the creation of a fantasy in reality.

The Narrative of Fantasy: the Pleasure Principle.

[The story of how you have pleased yourself.]

The baby feels hunger again (an increase of anxiety recurs); the baby sucks their own thumb and hallucinates receiving milk from a (m)other (a retreat into fantasy and auto-affection facilitated by a rehearsal of a memory); the thumb-sucking and hallucination together ease the baby's hunger (a decrease of anxiety).

The result: the pre-conscious re-writing of a memory and the repression of reality by a fantasy.

77

L__Other, ChiL.D__ι_(M)Other

THE NARRATIVE Of REALITY:
THE DEfERRAL Of
THE PLEASUre PRINCIPLE.

[The story of how you have made a [m)other please you.]

The baby feels hunger again (an increase of anxiety recurs); the baby sucks their own thumb and hallucinates milk from a (m)other (a retreat into fantasy and auto-affection facilitated by a rehearsal of a memory); the hunger doesn't subside (a further increase of anxiety); the baby cries in order to solicit a (m)other's attention, recalling that their cry had previously preceded their being fed (an attempt to solicit a (m)other's attention facilitated by a rehearsal of a memory); a (m)other arrives, attending to the rehearsed behavior, and gives the baby milk from her breast (an anxiety relieving encounter with a (m)other); the baby's hunger subsides (a decrease of anxiety).

The result: the self-conscious re-writing of a memory and the repression of a fantasy by reality.

THE NARRATIVE OF RE-CREATION.
THE BEYOND AFTER THE PLEASURE PRINCIPLE.

[The story of how you have made yourself [m]otherwise
in order to be pleased by a [m]other.]

The baby feels hunger again (an increase of anxiety recurs); the baby sucks their own thumb and hallucinates milk from a (m)other (a retreat into fantasy and auto-affection facilitated by a rehearsal of a memory); the hunger doesn't subside (a further increase of anxiety); the baby cries in order to solicit a (m)other's attention, recalling that their cry had previously preceded their being fed (an attempt to solicit a (m)other's attention facilitated by the rehearsal of a memory); a (m)other does not respond to the baby's cries (a further increase of anxiety); the baby attempts a new behavior in an to solicit a (m)other's attention (an attempt to solicit a (m)other's attention facilitated by an improvisation, a deviation from a memory); the (m)other arrives, attending to the improvised behavior, and gives the baby milk from her breast (an anxiety relieving encounter with the (m)other); hunger is relieved (a decrease of anxiety).

The result: the self-conscious over-writing of a memory and the re-creation of a fantasy in reality.

79

CHILD_HOOD
OR, BECOMING ONESELf

Insofar as we hunger, each and every one of us, is a child. Our birth mothers, wet nurses, or bottle feeders are our first (m)others but anyone, everyone, and everything that satisfies our hunger will become a (m)other to us. Our fathers and siblings become our (m)others. So do our friends, our lovers, our employers, our homelands (the "Motherland"), our governments (the "Nanny State"), and, of course, the natural world ("Mother Earth", "Mother Nature"). There are no limits to the entities human-and-non-human, animate-and-inanimate, singular-and-plural, that can become our (m)others.

(M}OTHEr_HOoD.
OR. BEING (M}OThErwISE

Insofar as we may satisfy the hunger of another, each and every one of us is also a (m)other, and anyone who turns to us for nourishment is our child. Our mothers, fathers, siblings, friends, and lovers become our children when we nourish them; our employers, homelands, and governments become our children when we nourish them; and the natural world too becomes our child when we nourish it. There are no limits to the entities human-and-non-human, animate-and-inanimate, singular-and-plural, that can become our children.

PLEASUrE ᵉᵗ PAIN.

Each and every one of us, being-in-ourselves, is child-and-mother, but each and everyone of us, being-for-others, either (i) assumes childhood to be pleased by others or (ii) assumes (m)otherhood to please others.

To assume childhood is to resolve oneself into a vessel and to take a measure from a flow, like the child nourished by the flow of milk. To find pleasure in childhood is either (i) to be nourished in moderation by letting a flow spill into and over you (and to find spurts of pleasure thereby), or (ii) to be nourished in excess by letting a flow carry you away in a flood (and to find oceanic pleasure thereby).

To assume (m)otherhood is to dissolve oneself into a flow and to be drawn in by a vessel, like the flow of milk that nourishes the child. To find pleasure in (m)otherhood is either (i) to nourish in moderation by spilling into and over a vessel (and to find spurts of pleasure thereby), or (ii) to nourish in excess by carrying away a vessel in a flood (and to find oceanic pleasure thereby).

At any given moment, one cannot pre-determine whether one will find pleasure in assuming childhood or in assuming (m)otherhood: one can only ever try to anticipate whether pleasure is to be found one way as opposed to another.

Affirmative pleasure, *the pleasure derived from effective action, is found when one anticipates correctly:*
- *When one assumes childhood in anticipation and then, subsequently, one is nourished by a counterpart who has assumed (m)otherhood; or*
- *When one assumes (m)otherhood in anticipation and then, subsequently, one is able to nourish a counterpart who has assumed childhood.*

Corrective pleasure, *the pleasure derived from effective re-action, is found when one anticipates incorrectly but corrects, assuming the opposite role:*
- *When one assumes childhood in anticipation and then, subsequently, after one's counterpart also assumes childhood, one abandons childhood for (m)otherhood and one nourishes one's counterpart; or*
- *When one assumes (m)otherhood in anticipation and then, subsequently, after one's counterpart also assumes (m)otherhood, one abandons (m)otherhood for childhood and is nourished by one's counterpart.*

Punitive pain, *the pain derived from ineffectiveness, is found whenever one anticipates wrongly. Punitive pain not only precedes every correction, it can also follow from correction.*
- *Every correction that follows a mistaken anticipation is itself an anticipation that one's counterpart will not also correct: if both counterparts correct, two corrections will cancel out and yield punitive pain rather corrective pleasure. In other words, punitive pain is re-doubled when both parties correct their course, and it is re-doubled when both parties stay their course. In order for correction to yield pleasure, one party must correct their course while the other party stays the course.*

83

INfANTILIZATION

Infantilization predisposes an individual to assume childhood over and against (m)otherhood by making an individual associate assuming (m)otherhood with pain and assuming childhood with pleasure. One who has been infantilized takes childhood for granted.

MATErₙALIZATION

Maternalization predisposes an individual to assume (m)otherhood over and against childhood by making an individual associate assuming childhood with pain and assuming (m)otherhood with pleasure. One who has been maternalized takes (m)otherhood for granted.

SIBLING RIVALrIES

To instigate a sibling rivalry is to predispose a (m)other to prioritize one child over and against another by associating the (m)othering of one child with pleasure and associating the (m)othering of another child with pain.

Patriarchal Powers

The power to infantilize, the power to maternalize, and the power to instigate sibling rivalries — these are patriarchal powers. We name these "patriarchal powers" because the archetypal patriarch, the "primal father", maternalizes his female partner(s), infantilizes himself, and instigates sibling rivalries so as to predispose his female partner(s) to prioritize him, as man-child, over and against everyone else, including his own offspring.

Counter -Patriarchal Powers

The power to resist infantilization, the power to resist maternalization, and the power to resist the instigation of sibling rivalries — these are counter-patriarchal powers.

SCHIZOPhRENICS

A schizophrenic is a child who composes a narrative of re-creation to make life pleasurable: the schizophrenic's life story is the story of their endeavors to make themself (m)otherwise in order to be pleased by (m)others. There are two kinds of schizophrenics: the ecstatic and the paranoiac

- *The* ecstatic *is the active schizophrenic who composes a narrative of re-creation revolving around a desire for affirmative pleasure.*
- *The* paranoiac *is the reactive schizophrenic who composes a narrative of re-creation revolving around a desire for corrective pleasure.*

Schizophrenics "do it with" (m)others. Whenever we speak of the paranoiac and the ecstatic, we ought to also speak of the (m)others that enable and are enabled by them: the (m)others of paranoia and the (m)others of ecstasy. Schizophrenics and their (m)others exercise counter-patriarchal powers when they "do it together", resisting infantilization, maternalization, and the instigation of sibling rivalries.

FETISHIST-PROVOCATEURS

A fetishist-provocateur is a child who composes a narrative of reality to make life pleasurable: the fetishist-provocateur's life story is the story of their endeavors to make (m)others please them. There are two kinds of fetishist-provocateur: the narcissist and the pervert.

- The **narcissist** is the active fetishist-provocateur who composes a narrative of reality revolving around a desire for affirmative pleasure.
- The **pervert** is the reactive fetishist-provocateur who composes a narrative of reality revolving around a desire for corrective pleasure.

Fetishist-provocateurs disable themselves in order to make (m)others "do it for them". Thus, whenever we speak of the narcissist and the pervert, we ought to also speak of the (m)others that they enable: (m)others of narcissism and the (m)others of perversion. Fetishist-provocateurs and their (m)others are the agents and patients of infantilization and maternalization. The narcissist is the agent of maternalization and their (m)others are their patients, but, at the same time, the narcissist is both agent and patient of their own infantilization. By contrast, the pervert is the patient of infantilization and their (m)other is the agent of their infantilization, but, at the same time, the (m)other of the pervert is both agent and patient of their own maternalization.

87

FANTASIST-MASTURBATORS

A fantasist-masturbator is a child who composes a narrative of fantasy to make life pleasurable: the fantasist-masturbator's life story is the story of their endeavors to please themselves. There are two kinds of fantasist-masturbators: the hysteric and the obsessive.

- *The* **obsessive** *is the active fantasist-masturbator who composes a narrative of fantasy revolving around a desire for affirmative pleasure.*
- *The* **hysteric** *is the reactive fantasist-masturbator who composes a narrative of fantasy revolving around a desire for corrective pleasure.*

Fantasist-masturbators disable (m)others who would "do it with them" or "do it for them" in order to "do it themselves". Thus, whenever we speak of the obsessive and the hysteric, we ought to also speak of the (m)others that the obsessive and the hysteric disable: the (m)others of paranoia, the (m)others of ecstasy, (m)others of narcissism and the (m)others of perversion. Fantasist-masturbators are the patients of both infantilizations and sibling rivalries: they are the frustrated rival siblings who, having fallen out of their (m)other's favor, disavow their desire for a (m)other.

MASturBATory FANTASIES

A fantasist-masturbator can play (m)other to themself in and through four different kinds of masturbatory fantasies

- *The obsessive fantasist-masturbator retreats into* **affirmative fantasies** *either (i) playing (m)other of ecstasy to themself in an ecstatic fantasy or (ii) playing (m)other of narcissism to themself in an narcissistic fantasy.*

- *The hysteric fantasist-masturbator retreats into* **corrective fantasies** *either (i) playing (m)other of paranoia to themself in a paranoid fantasy or (ii) playing (m)other of perversion to themself in a perverse fantasy.*

Supₚly et Demand.

To assume childhood is to assume the role of the consumer: to **demand** that (m)others supply sensations. To assume (m)otherhood is to assume the role of the producer: to **supply** sensations.

- One finds **punitive pain in childhood** when one demands sensations only to find no (m)others that will supply them.

- One finds **punitive pain in [m]otherhood** when on finds no demand for the sensations that one supplies.

- One finds **affirmative pleasure in childhood** when one demands sensations and finds (m)others that will supply them.

- One finds **affirmative pleasure in [m]otherhood** when one finds a demand for the sensations that one supplies.

- One finds **corrective pleasure in childhood** when one finds a (m)other who will supply sensations that satisfy one's demand for sensations, as a child, but only after having found no demand for the sensations that one would supply as a (m)other.

- One finds **corrective pleasure in [m]otherhood** when one finds a demand for the sensations that one supplies, as a (m)other, but only after having found no (m)other to supply the sensations that one demands as a child.

The schizophrenic is the child who works with their (m)other to satisfy their demand for sensations—the **engaged consumer** *who collaborates with the producer on the design, manufacture, and development of a satisfying product or service.*

- *The ecstatic seeks affirmative pleasure via a (m)other that also seeks affirmative pleasure.*
- *The paranoid seeks corrective pleasure via a (m)other that also seeks corrective pleasure.*

The fetishist-provocateur is the child who does nothing but demand that (m)others satisfy them—the **idle consumer** *who demands a satisfying product or service from a producer but either cannot or will not collaborate with the producer on the design, manufacture, and development of the product or service.*

- *The narcissist seeks affirmative pleasure via a (m)other that seeks corrective pleasure.*
- *The pervert seeks corrective pleasure via a (m)other that seeks affirmative pleasure.*

The fantasist-masturbator is the child who would satisfy their own demand for sensations and disavows (m)others who would satisfy them— the **anti-consumer** *who would produce what they consume and consume what they produce.*

- *The obsessive fantasist-masturbator seeks affirmative pleasure by retreating into ecstatic or narcissistic fantasies.*
- *The hysterical fantasist-masturbator seeks corrective pleasure by retreating into paranoid or perverse fantasies.*

BECOMING
SENSITIVE
BEING
SENSATIONAL

All pleasures and pains are derived from and refer back to the senses.

The pleasures and pains of childhood are found in becoming sensitive, in receiving sensations. For example, the assumption of childhood by the movie-viewer is a becoming eyes-and-ears.

The pleasures and pains of (m)otherhood are found in being sensational, in supplying sensations. For example, the assumption of (m)otherhood by the movie-star is a being seen-and-heard.

The list of becomings-sensitive and beings-sensational on the next page is suggestive, not exhaustive. It features some of the most prevalent becomings-sensitive and beings-sensational, and of the becomings-sensitive and beings-sensational not listed are superpositions of those that are listed here.

Becoming-Eyes
Being-Seen
Receiving/Supplying Scopic Sensations

Becoming-Lips
Being-Kissed
Receiving/Supplying Osculatory Sensations

Becoming-Ears
Being-Heard
Receiving/Supplying Aural Sensations

Becoming-Tongue
Being-Tasted
Receiving/Supplying Gustatory Sensations

Becoming-Skin
Being-Felt
Receiving/Supplying Tactile Sensations

Becoming-Teeth
Being-Bitten
Receiving/Supplying Masticatory Sensations

Becoming-Nose
Being-Smelled
Receiving/Supplying Aromatic Sensations

Becoming-Guts
Being-Digested
Receiving/Supplying Visceral Sensations

Becoming-Anus
Being-Shit
Receiving/Supplying Anal Sensations

Becoming-Hands
Being-Handled
Receiving/Supplying Manual Sensations

Becoming-Genitals
Being-Fucked
Receiving/Supplying Sexual Sensations

Becoming-Nipples
Being-a-Suckling
Receiving/Supplying Mammary Sensations

Becoming-Muscles
Being-Hefted
Receiving/Supplying Musculatory Sensations

Becoming-Lungs
Being-Asphyxiating
Receiving/Supplying Respiratory Sensations

THE SENTIMENTS

The sentiments are expressions of desire. The sentiments as "expressions" of desire are to be distinguished from sense organs as "contents" of desire and from sensations as "matters" of desire.

The list of sentiments below is not exhaustive, but all the sentiments that are not listed below are superpositions of the sentiments that are listed below.

- **Sadness** is an expression of a perverse desire, a desire to find corrective pleasure by relenting to a reality that pains oneself but pleases (m)others. (M)others of perversion desire to enable sadness, and their desire to do so is called pity. In sum, (m)others of perversion are pitying (m)others, and **sadness is the pervert's desire for pity and pitying (m)others.**

- **Complacency** is an expression of a narcissistic desire, a desire to find affirmative pleasure by relenting to a reality that pleases oneself but pains (m)others. (M)others of narcissism desire to enable complacency, and their desire to do so is called meekness. In sum, (m)others of narcissism are meek (m)others, and **complacency is the narcissist's desire for meekness and meek (m)others.**

- **Fear** *is an expression of a paranoid desire, a desire to find corrective pleasure by re-creating a corrective fantasy in reality with the help of (m) others. (M)others of paranoia desire to be enabled by and to be enablers of fear, and their desire to enable and be enabled by fear is* **cruelty.** *In sum, (m)others of paranoia are cruel (m)others, and* **fear is the paranoid's desire for cruelty and cruel (m)others.**

- **Wonder** *is an expression of an ecstatic desire, a desire to find affirmative pleasure by re-creating an affirmative fantasy in reality with the help of (m)others. (M)others of ecstasy desire to be enabled by and to be enablers of wonder, and their desire to enable and be enabled by wonder is* **love.** *In sum,(m)others of ecstasy are loving (m)others, and* **wonder is the ecstatic's desire for love and loving (m)others.**

- **Anger** *is an expression of a hysterical desire, a desire to find corrective pleasure by retreating from reality into a corrective fantasy. The hysteric's anger is directed towards (m)others that they disable when enabling themselves. As such, the hysteric's* **anger is the hysteric's shame at and disavowal of their desire for cruelty and/or pity from (m)others.**

- **Disgust** *is an expression of an obsessive desire, a desire to find affirmative pleasure by retreating from reality into an affirmative fantasy. The obsessive's disgust is directed towards (m)others that they disable when enabling themselves. As such, the obsessive's* **disgust is the obsessive's shame at and disavowal of their desire for love and/or meekness from (m)others.**

*9*5

An Examined Life

To know oneself is to know when, where, how, why, with whom, and for whom one might become disposed towards each and every possible sensation and sentiment that one is capable of affecting and being affected by.

To live an examined life is to live in order to know-oneself and to seek answers to the following questions:

- *When, where, how, why, and with-and-for whom might I become disposed to anger, disgust, sadness, complacency, fear, wonder, pity, meekness, cruelty, and love?*
- *When, where, how, why, and with-and-for whom might I become disposed towards either affecting or being affected by certain sights, sounds, smells, tastes, textures, etc.?*

LIVED EXPERIMENTS AND THOUGHT EXPERIMENTS

A thought experiment *is a constative essay in and through which one proposes know-what, know-how, know-why, know-where, know-when, know-where, and know-whom-with-and-for. Thought experiments propose knowledge and, as such, all thought experiments involve propositions and logics. This means that only symbolic species perform thought experiments.*

A lived experiment *is a performative essay in and through which one substantiates know-what, know-how, know-why, know-where, know-when, know-where, and know-whom-with-and-for. The lived experiment substantiates knowledge: all social species, not just symbolic species, perform lived experiments. Symbolic species differ from other social species by the fact that their lived experiments are occasionally informed by thought experiments.*

An Un_Examined Life

There are those who take propositional knowledge for granted. There are those who claim to have know-what, know-how, know-why, know-where, know-when, know-where, and know-whom-with-and-for, but who have not and will not substantiate their claims. Such claimants believe that their knowledge transcends substantiation: they believe that their failure to substantiate their knowledge does not point to the fact that their knowledge is lacking but, rather, points to the fact their sense organs, sensations, and sentiments are lacking. In sum, they claim that they have knowledge of a reality that transcends the senses and the sentiments. Those who make such claims are those who live unexamined lives.

An unexamined life is a life that disdains substantial knowledge and favors propositional knowledge. As such, an unexamined life is a form of life found only amongst symbolic species: an unexamined life is not possible for creatures lacking propositional knowledge.

THE AfFLICTEd et ThE CURED

Unexamined living is the affliction of the symbolic species.
Proposing that there exists knowledge that cannot be substantiated,
the afflicted claims, "I know that there is something wrong with
me." And the afflicted goes on to say of others, "I know that there is
something wrong with them."

Examined living is the cure for the affliction of the symbolic species.
Always endeavoring to substantiate their knowledge, the cured
claims, "There cannot be anything right or wrong with me; I can
only ever be right or wrong about myself." And the cured goes on to
say of others, "There cannot be anything right or wrong with others;
others can only ever be right or wrong about themselves."

Dispositions Are not Afflictions

Narcissism, perversion, ecstasy, paranoia, obsession, and hysteria are dispositions, not afflictions. The surest sign that someone is afflicted, living an unexamined life, is that someone claims a dispositions is an affliction.

There is nothing bad about being disposed to narcissism, perversion, ecstasy, paranoia, catatonia, obsession, or hysteria; there is only something bad about the claim that one is badly disposed.

In other words, there are no bad dispositions, only bad situations with respect to a preferred disposition.

If one finds oneself disposed to perversion, there is nothing bad about one's perverse disposition. There is only something bad about the claim that one ought to be disposed otherwise. This is not to say, however, that one shouldn't prefer to be disposed otherwise. This is only to say that one's preference for a disposition other than one's current disposition does not make one's current disposition a bad disposition. Rather, it only makes one's current situation the bad situation with respect to one's preferred disposition. A preference for a disposition is motivation to extricate oneself from bad situations for one's preferred disposition and to find situations that yield one's preferred disposition. For example, if I prefer to be disposed to ecstasy but find myself disposed to perversion, I should be motivated to extricate myself from situations that dispose me to perversion and to seek situations that would dispose me to ecstasy, but I should not condemn myself for being disposed to perversion given my current situation.

Examined living is part and parcel of any and all attempts to extricate oneself from bad situations and to find better situations and, as such, attempts to find better situations cure the affliction of unexamined living. What's more, whether one succeeds or fails at finding a better fitting situation, one's attempt to do so will cure the affliction. Of course, one wants to succeed in one's attempt, but it is the attempt that cures, regardless of the success or failure of the attempt.

HoStiLity,
CHArILT Y,
et INdIſFErENCe

If others near and dear to me prefer to be disposed to paranoia while I prefer to be disposed to ecstasy, and these others succeed at finding situations that dispose them to paranoia while I fail at finding situations that dispose me to ecstasy, I should not begrudge these others their successes and condemn their preferred dispositions for being the "wrong" dispositions. Rather, I should acknowledge their successful attempts and find whatever inspiration I can in their successes.

To be **hostile** *is to deny others their successes and to condemn others'* *preferred dispositions. One engenders the affliction of unexamined* *living in both oneself and others when one is hostile, and one makes* *foes thereby.*

To be **charitable** *is to acknowledge others' successful attempts and* *to find inspiration in them. One makes kin and cures the affliction of* *unexamined living by being charitable.*

To be **indifferent** *is to be neither hostile nor charitable, to* *acknowledge others' successes, yes, but to find their successes* *uninspiring. One makes oneself a stranger by being indifferent.*

ETHICISTS and MORALISTS

Being hostile and making foes spreads the affliction of unexamined living.

Being indifferent and making oneself a stranger neither spreads nor cures the affliction of unexamined living, but it does prevent the spread of the affliction.

Only being charitable and making kin cures the affliction of unexamined living.

Ethicists *are those who claim that, when making kin is not an option, it is better to become indifferent and to make oneself a stranger. In other words, ethicists prefer to make strangers as opposed to foes.*

Moralists *are those who claim that, when making kin is not an option, it is better to become hostile and to make foes. In other words, moralists prefer to make foes as opposed to strangers*

POSTLUDE:

ON ETHICS

(BEYOND MORALITY)

oNE.

Moralists insist upon one notion of what is good.
Ethicists, by contrast, insist that one notion of what is good
is always one of many notions, and that no one notion is objectively
higher, truer, or more desirable than any other.
Ethicists acknowledge and respect the fact that different individuals and groups
will have different notions at different times
about what is good.
What's more, and here's the rub, ethicists also acknowledge and respect moralists—
that is to say, in other words, that ethicists acknowledge and respect
the fact that moralists can and will insist that their notion
is the highest, truest, and most desirable of all.

two.

One can be certain that another person is a moralist when that person
considers declaring and waging war against
"bad actors", "bad behaviors", and "false goods".
Insisting upon one notion of what is
the highest, truest, and most desirable of all goods,
moralists can convince themselves that they do good
by waging war against those who insist otherwise.
They can convince themselves that it is good
to force others to abandon their native, indigenous notion of the good,
to force others submit to a foreign, colonizing notion.
The moralist considers declaring and waging war against other moralists
over disagreements about what is
the highest, truest, and most desirable good
And the moralist considers declaring and waging war against ethicists
who do not acknowledge any good as being objectively
higher, truer, or more desirable than any other.

THrEE.

One can be certain that a person is an ethicist when a person refuses
to consider declaring and waging war against
"bad actors", "bad behaviors", and "false goods".
It is undoubtedly true that ethicists will consider moralists
"bad actors" and "badly behaved"
when moralists choose to wage war for the sake of
the highest, truest, and most desirable good.
But ethicists do not care to wage war against moralists for this reason.
Ethicists do obviously have to defend themselves against moralists
who would force ethicists to submit,
but ethicists only really care to negotiate peace
with and amongst ethicists and moralists.
Moralists always have the option
to either wage war or to negotiate peace
in order to advance the highest, truest, and most desirable good.
Ethicists only ever have the option to negotiate peace
so that their good may coexist alongside other goods.
The ethicist never launches preemptive strikes,
and war is always forced upon the ethicist
by the aggression of the moralist.
The moralist, thus, has two free hands when it comes to doing good,
the hand that wages war and the hand that negotiates peace.
The ethicist only has one free hand,
the hand that negotiates peace;
ethics is the art of doing good with only one free hand.

*ƒ*0**U**R.

Moralities are justifications for waging a war against
> *"bad actors", "bad behaviors", and "false goods"*
>> *in the name of the highest, truest, and most desirable good.*

Ethics are tactics for negotiating a peace
> *that would enable many different notions of the good to coexist*
>> *alongside one another.*

Ethicists eschew war in and through the practice of ethics,
> *but this does not mean that ethicists shy away from*
>> *confrontations and battles.*

The ethicist recognizes that one peace
> *can be better or worse than another peace.*

The worst peace is the one which allows one notion of the good
> *to override and overrule over all others.*

The best peace is the one which allows all notions of the good
> *a sphere of "relative autonomy"*
>> *without allowing any one notion to override and overrule*
>>> *any other notion.*

Going further, the ethicist recognizes that, on many occasions,
> *in order to negotiate a better peace,*
>> *one must be able to contend in confrontations and battles.*

Indeed, all ethics involve tactics for contending in skirmishes
> *in order to negotiate a better peace.*

At the same time, however, all ethics will also involve
> *deescalation tactics*
>> *so as to prevent skirmishes from escalating into wars.*

APPENDIX:

THE ARTIST AS VISUAL VALUE CREATOR

It is one thing to know that one wants to become an artist. It is another thing to know what role one wants to play in society in and through becoming an artist. Assuming that I know the former, that I know that I want to become an artist, this text is an attempt to learn the latter, to learn what role I want to play in society in and through becoming an artist.

Taking my lead from William Deresiewicz's book, The Death of the Artist, *I will begin this text by considering the four roles that Deresiewicz claims the artist has played in society over the course of history. In order of historical appearance, these four roles are that of the master artisan, that of the solitary genius, that of the credentialed professional, and that of the creative entrepreneur.*

- *The* **master artisan** *is the "antiquated" figure of the traditional artist: the figure of the artist as inheritor, keeper, reviver, and transmitter of a refined craft. To play the role of the master artisan is to act as if art is to be made by the craftsman who respects and reveres a tradition and is retained in the service of aristocratic or priestly guardians of tradition.*

- *The* **solitary genius** *is the "modern" figure of the romantic artist: the figure of the artist in revolt against the ideology of progress but in league with the ideology of individualism. The solitary genius maintains that the idea of progress is, by turns, too conservative and too destructive to promote the individual, no matter whether the idea of progress is realized via a bureaucratic meritocracy or via the wisdom of the crowd assembled in the market. To play the solitary genius is to act as if art is to be made by the individual on a lonely quest to achieve transcendence and made for the sake of the individual's lonely quest.*

- *The* **credentialed professional** *is the "high modern" figure of the meritocratic artist: the figure of the artist as technical expert or specialist. To play the credentialed professional is to act as if art is to be made by specialized technicians employed or contracted by public or private interests.*

- *The* **creative entrepreneur** *is the "late modern" figure of the capitalistic artist: the figure of the artist as huckster and hustler selling themself on the market. To play the creative entrepreneur is to act as if art can be made by anyone who can afford to make it and made for anyone who can afford to pay for it.*

111

As Deresiewicz notes, there hasn't been clear linear progression with respect to these four successive roles: it hasn't been the case that each successive role has outmoded the previous roles. There were, and still are, overlaps between these four successive roles—"long transitions, mixed and marginal cases, anticipations and survivals." Today, however, it is clearly the case that the creative entrepreneur is the figure of the artist on the rise, the figure coming into its own and setting the terms and trends in art making.

The rise of the creative entrepreneur as the dominant figure of the artist is a distressing fact for me, because I know for certain that I do not want to become a creative entrepreneur. Certainly, the gumption of the creative entrepreneur has something to be said for it in comparison to the servility of the master artisan, the gloominess of the solitary genius, and the careerism of the credentialed professional. At the same, however, the creative entrepreneur is a reactive figure of the artist, having emerged in reaction to political economic conditions, following the decline of the post–World War II social democratic state which promoted professionalism and thanks to the rise of the post-Cold War neo-liberal state which promotes entrepreneurship. That being said, however, the roles of the master artisan, the solitary genius, and the credentialed professional are no less reactive roles from my perspective, also having emerged in reaction to political economic conditions. The reactiveness of the creative entrepreneur is only more readily apparent and appalling to me because I am so palpably aware of the conditions that the creative entrepreneur is reacting to.

In considering what role I would play as an artist in society, I have been tempted most by the role of the solitary genius. This is because I want to believe, and those who have played the role of the solitary genius would have me believe, that the solitary genius's retreat from the world is not reactive. The more I consider the matter, however, the more I recognize that the solitary genius only emerged after artists of sublimity and subtlety lost their social bearings following the decline of the aristocratic and religious patronage systems, and that this loss of social bearings forced artists of sublimity and subtlety to become increasingly more "self-reliant". Indeed, upon closer scrutiny, I have found that the figure of the solitary genius emerged as a valorization of "self-reliance" in reaction to the decline of the structures that supported the master artisan, just as the figure of the creative entrepreneur emerged as a valorization of "self-reliance" in reaction to the decline of the structures supporting credentialed professionals.

As I see it now, the narrative of the emergence of the four roles for the artist that Deresiewicz identifies runs as follows. The figure of the master artisan emerged as a reaction to the political economy of traditional aristocratic societies, and the figure of the credentialed professional emerged as a reaction to the political economy of bourgeois meritocratic societies. In the interregnum between the decline of traditional aristocratic societies and the rise of bourgeois meritocratic societies, the solitary genius emerged as a reaction to the political economic struggle between traditional aristocrats and the bourgeois meritocrats. Today, prevailing bourgeois meritocratic societies have been thrown into turmoil by political economic crises of their own making, and the creative entrepreneur has emerged in reaction to the turmoil. Insofar as there are some remnants of traditional aristocratic societies today, there are still master artisans. Insofar as some artists still live between traditional aristocracies and bourgeois meritocracies, there are still solitary geniuses. Insofar as bourgeois meritocracies still have the strength to confront the crises that they currently face, there are still credentialed professional artists. That being said, however, insofar as the political economy of our age is defined by bourgeois meritocracies in crisis, the arts of our age are defined by the figure of the creative entrepreneur.

The allure of the solitary genius stems from the fact that the champions of solitary geniuses have romanticized their quests for transcendence so as to keep audiences from attending to profound tragedies that precede, exceed, and succeed their quests for transcendence. Let us never fail to recognize that genuine genius is genial as opposed to solitary: a genius must have community and customs to transform in order to prove their genius. Genius only appears to be solitary to those who do not recognize that a genius only withdraws from their community and customs in order to regard them from a distance, hoping to return to them and transform them. The figure of the solitary genius is a tragic figure because the solitary genius is the genius who withdraws from their community and customs, regards them from distance, and discovers that they can never return to and transform their community and customs because their community and customs are terminally ill and can no longer endure great transformations. Indeed, the solitary genius only endeavors to transcend their community and customs because they cannot return to and transform them. More and more, I find that the art of solitary genius is but an expression of grief at a loss of community and customs, and I find that the art of the solitary genius can be classified according to the stage of grief in which it was made: in denial, anger, bargaining, depression, or acceptance. This is to say, in other words, that one properly becomes a solitary genius by bearing witness to the death of one's community and customs and by creating art that expresses one's grief at this loss, whether in denial, anger, bargaining, depression, or acceptance. In sum, the solitary genius is the figure of the artist in mourning over a genuine and profound loss.

Going further, I also find that the death of communities and customs is the thread that connects the progression from the master artisan to the solitary genius, from the solitary genius to the credentialed professional, and from the credentialed professional to the creative entrepreneur. The rise of bourgeois meritocracies, with their ideologies of individualism and progress, has meant the death of the genuine communities and customs guarded by aristocracies and priesthoods. With the decline of genuine communities and customs, the master artisan was cut adrift and lost their social bearings, becoming the solitary genius grieving the decline of community and customs. For better or for worse, the credentialed professional, who succeeded the solitary genius, found solace in the ersatz community of "the profession" and the ersatz customs of "techniques". Now, of course, the ersatz community of "the profession" and the ersatz customs of "techniques" are in decline, and the creative entrepreneur is the figure of the artist who oscillates between denial and bargaining with respect to their grief at the decline of ersatz communities and ersatz customs.

What is most distasteful to me about the credentialed professional is the fact that the credentialed professional settles for ersatz community and ersatz customs. What is most distasteful to me about the creative entrepreneur is the fact that the creative entrepreneur grieves the loss of ersatz community and ersatz customs without ever having endured and grieved the loss of genuine community and genuine customs. The figure of the solitary genius, as opposed to the creative entrepreneur, is so appealing to me because the solitary genius grieves the loss of something genuine as opposed to a substitute, but the solitary genius is equally unappealing for never proving their genius in a genuine and genial manner. The master artisan's appeal for me is their realization of genuine and genial genius in and through their transformations of genuine communities and customs, but the master artisan is equally unappealing to me because they take their genuine communities and customs for granted when I cannot.

Given that none of the historical roles for the artists appeal to me, I have struggled with the question, "What is to be done?" I shall spare you an account of my research and struggles, for these are detailed elsewhere. Instead, I will offer you the results of my research and struggles, and I will ask you to consult my other writings if my conclusions appeal to you. To put it briefly, I believe that there is a fifth role for the artist available to me. It is a role that is never properly recognized by historians because it is, in a sense, a para-historical role: a role that does not make history but breaks (with) history. This fifth role, which I would make my own, is the role of the value creator.

Unlike the figure of the creative entrepreneur who grieves the loss of ersatz communities and customs, unlike the credentialed professional who is precious about the ersatz communities and customs they maintain, unlike the figure of the solitary genius who grieves the loss of genuine communities and customs, and unlike the master artisan who takes genuine communities and customs for granted— **the value creator, taking great care and taking nothing for granted, is the artist who [re-]creates genuine communities and genuine customs in order to transform them with and through their genius.**

Restating what I have already stated for greater emphasis, the value creator, as part and parcel of their artistic practice, is also tasked with contributing to the (re-)creation of a genuine community and genuine customs that will yield sensibilities and understandings that complement their art. In (re-)creating genuine communities and customs, the value creator hearkens back to the "dark precursor" of the artist, the figure that preceded even that of the master artisan: the figure of the shaman. Indeed, to borrow two concepts from Friedrich Schiller, the figure of the shaman could be called the "naïve" value creator, and the figure of the self-conscious value creator could be called the "sentimental" shaman. The self-conscious value creator, as "sentimental" shaman, (re-)creates genuine community and genuine customs self-reflectively, having had to consciously recognize how and why it is that they need genuine community and genuine customs. The shaman, as "naïve" value creator, creates genuine community and genuine custom spontaneously, without self-reflection, without ever having to consciously recognize how and why it is they need community and customs.

The practice of the shaman, or the naïve value creator, spontaneously contributes to the making of the genuine community that I refer to as the shaman's "folk" and to the making of genuine customs that I refer to as "folkways". The practice of self-conscious value creator, or the sentimental shaman, self-reflectively contributes to the making of a genuine community of what I refer to as "fellow travelers" and to the making of genuine customs that I refer to as "getaways". *

---

* *The term "getaway", from the verbal phrase "get away" and meaning "an escape", arose originally in fox hunting and first referred to the manner in which foxes eluded hunters and their dogs. The term was soon after used to refer to the manner in which prisoners and criminals eluded the authorities and their agents, and it has more recently come to refer to travel for pleasure.*

The activity of value creators with respect to communities and customs is to be distinguished from:

- The activity of the creative entrepreneur, for whom brand building involves contributing to the making of second-order ersatz communities called "networks" and to the making of second-order ersatz customs called "gimmicks";

- The activity of the credentialed professional, for whom career building involves contributing to the making of first-order ersatz communities called "professions" and to the making of first-order ersatz customs called "techniques"; and

- The activity of the master artisan, for whom becoming a master involves contributing to the making of the genuine communities found in traditional "workshops", "performance troupes", "aristocratic retinues", "religious orders", and "craftsmen's guilds", and to the making of the genuine customs that are collectively called "crafts".

The solitary genius is not distinguished in this regard, because the solitary genius does not contribute to the making of community or customs, genuine or ersatz, but "transcends" the making of community and custom. That being said, however, it should be noted here the ordeals of solitary genius have often motivated artists to become value creators. Indeed, the solitary genius who has reached the final stage of grief, acceptance, inevitably becomes a value creator.

So, first, let us distinguish the activity of the master artisan. The activity of the master artisan differs from that of the value creator in that the master artisan does not create new values but, rather, upholds an established hierarchy of values. This is because the master artisan is the servant of aristocracies and priesthoods.

Aristocracies and priesthoods fear and fight against value creators because the creation of new values is always a revaluation of existing hierarchies of values. Aristocracies and priesthoods acquire their authority by exploiting existing hierarchies of values and maintain their authority by maintaining existing hierarchies of values. Revaluations of values effected by value creators threaten not only to expose the ways in which aristocracies and priesthoods exploit existing hierarchies of values but, more profoundly still, revaluations threaten to overturn existing hierarchies of values and to topple aristocracies and priesthoods.

The master artisan is the figure of the artist who has been tamed by aristocracies and priesthoods. The communities and customs that the master artisan contributes to are communities and customs that uphold existing hierarchies of values and that maintain the authority of aristocracies and priesthoods. That being said, however, insofar as any and every existing hierarchy of values was initially the work of a value creator, it could be said that the master artisan respects and reveres certain acts of value creation. Indeed, some master artisans respect and revere acts of value creation so much that they themselves attempt to re-create acts of value creation in homage to original acts of value creation, and, in so doing, they wind up becoming value creators themselves.

The ArtiSt - VaLue CreatOr

Whereas the master artisan is the faithful servant of established hierarchies of values, the credentialed professional and the creative entrepreneur are mercenaries and opportunistic servants of established hierarchies of values. Whereas the master artisan respected and revered the acts of value creation that created the hierarchy of values that they upheld, the credentialed professional and the creative entrepreneur believe that one hierarchy of values can be exchanged for another, one act of value creation can be exchanged for another, and different hierarchies of values should compete with one another for the services that the artist provide in upholding them. For the credentialed professional and the creative entrepreneur, no one act of value creation and no one hierarchy of values is to be respected and revered in and of itself, what is to be respected and revered is "building a career" or "building a brand", and acts of value creation and hierarchies of values are better or worse in light of whether they promise "career opportunities" or to "promote the brand".

The credentialed professional, who "builds a career" by specializing, makes a calculated mercenary choice regarding what existing hierarchies of values will profit them most and sticks with their choice to become an expert at what they do, for better or for worse, . The creative entrepreneur, for whom a "brand refresh" is about diversification, continually makes new mercenary choices regarding what hierarchies of values will profit them attending to ever changing market conditions, never really becoming expert at anything. Like the master artisan, however, neither the credentialed professional nor creative entrepreneur sets out to create new values, as there is no profit in the creation of values but only in servicing existing hierarchies of values. Then again, however, like the solitary genius's extreme grief and master artisan's extreme reverence can transform them into value creators, the extreme specialization of credentialed professionalism and extreme novelty of creative entrepreneurship may also produce value creators under extreme conditions. The credentialed professional may not set out to create new values in and through specialization but some wind up doing so through over-specialization. The creative entrepreneur may not set out to create new values in and through their perpetual search for new gimmicks but some wind up doing so when they run out of new gimmicks.

Indeed, I find that many artists become value creators without ever intending to. Reading the biographies of artists who have become value creators can lead one to believe that the road to becoming a value creator is initially characterized by a becoming-artisan, or a becoming-solitary, or a becoming-professional, or a becoming-entrepreneurial. The biography of master artisan turned value creator suggests that paying homage to original acts of value creation is the sure road to value creation. The biography of the solitary genius turned value creator suggests that the quest for "transcendence" is the sure road to value creation. The biography of the credentialed professional turned value creator suggests that overspecialization is the sure road to value creation. Lastly, the biography of the creative entrepreneur turned value creator suggests that refusing to use the same gimmick twice is the sure road to value creation. Upon closer inspection, however, I find that these suggestions are all mistaken valorizations of the indignities and ordeals that have characterized particular journeys to becoming value creators. Indeed, I firmly believe that an artist's journey to becoming a value creator needn't be characterized by the servility of the master artisan, nor by the gloominess of the solitary genius, nor by the careerism of the credentialed professional, nor by the gumption of the creative entrepreneur. It is my belief that journeys characterized by such indignities and ordeals are journeys that have been hindered by reactive forces that are marshaled against those who would become value creators.

Indeed, as I understand them now, "folkways", the genuine customs created by naïve value creators, are unconscious vehicles of eluding and escaping indignities and ordeals that would hinder value creation; and "getaways", the genuine customs created by self-conscious value creators, are self-conscious vehicles for eluding and escaping the indignities and ordeals that would hinder value creation. In line with this, I now understand that the "folk" of a naïve value creator are fellow naïve value creators who unconsciously work together to practice folkways that undermine the formation of aristocracies, priesthoods, meritocracies, and markets. Ay, and I now understand that the fellow travelers of a self-conscious value creator are fellow self-conscious value creators who work together to make getaways, escaping the indignities and ordeals that established aristocracies, priesthoods, meritocracies, and markets would impose on their journeys.

I must stress here that "folkways" are *unconscious* vehicles of value creation and that "getaways" are *self-conscious* vehicles of value creation. Just like the unconscious defenses of the body and mind prove most effective against most physical and mental illnesses up to a critical point but must be supplemented by self-conscious efforts beyond a critical point; folkways as an unconscious defense against the formation of aristocracies, priesthoods, meritocracies, and markets are effective up to a point, but they must be supplemented by self-conscious getaways beyond a critical point. In other words, the folkways of naïve value creators no longer suffice to escape indignities and ordeals once aristocracies, priesthoods, meritocracies, and markets have firmly established themselves, and only the getaways self-conscious value creators can enable us to escape the indignities and ordeals that established aristocracies, priesthoods, meritocracies, and markets impose us on upon our journeys to become value creators.

Folkways tend to accumulate and become weighty over time, and aristocracies and priesthoods work to transform accumulated masses of folkways into iron balls at the end of chains that bind and weigh down anyone with an impetus for value creation. Indeed, aristocracies and priesthoods are only able to establish themselves by promoting the accumulation of folkways and by exploiting the weightiness of accumulated folkways. In so doing, aristocracies and priesthoods force artists to become master artisans, to hone folkways into crafts and weigh themselves down with unwieldy masses of folkways in masochistic shows of deference to aristocracies and priesthoods. Indeed, the master artisan is none other than the artist chained to burdensome folkways, and the master artisan's craft is none other than the chain that binds them to burdensome folkways.

Unlike folkways, getaways are self-consciously designed to avoid ever accumulating and becoming weighty burdens. Getaways are maximally ephemeral: they dissipate rather than accumulate. That being said, however, though getaways can easily avoid being honed into crafts by being ephemeral, their ephemerality is exploited by professional techniques and by entrepreneurial gimmicks. This is to say, in other words, that self-conscious value creators struggle more with meritocracies and markets than they do with aristocracies and priesthoods.

Meritocracies aim to create misery for artists by placing them in double binds that are more difficult for them to escape. The credentialed professional is the artist who studies getaways in order to continually create double binds. Escaping the chain of craft that bound the master artisan to the iron ball of accumulated folkways is child's play in comparison to escaping the double binds of technique that the credentialed professional creates. The double binds created by the credentialed professional cannot be avoided by means of ephemerality alone because they aim to transform ephemerality from a liberty into a liability. Faced with the double bind of technique on one side and craft on the other, the value creator must learn to play ephemerality with and against weightiness if they are to escape the double bind of craftsmanship and professionalism.

Whereas the credentialed professional makes escape increasingly more difficult for the artist, the creative entrepreneur makes a mockery of escape. The creative entrepreneur is the "escape artist" who turns escape into a gimmicky spectacle, making a mockery of the getaways of self-conscious value creators. The creative entrepreneur doesn't know how to make a genuine getaway and doesn't really want to: they only want to feign entertaining getaways to amass a following. Whereas the value creator's genuine getaways are designed to be maximally ephemeral, the creative entrepreneur's feigned getaways are drawn out in a spectacular fashion to keep audiences spellbound. From this, it follows that the creative entrepreneur's less genuine but more belabored achievements tend to earn far more esteem and recognition than the more genuine but also more ephemeral achievements of the value creator, much to the value creator's chagrin.

So, how does the value creator escape not only the burdens of craft but also the miseries of credentialed professionalism and the mockeries of creative entrepreneurship? I cannot pretend to have answered this question fully but I do believe that I have the beginnings of a suggestive answer.

The Artist - Value Creator

First and foremost, and above all else, I believe that value creators must endeavor to find each other. The mantra of value creation ought to be, "You will never escape on your own!" Stated negatively, the value creator must not succumb to the lures of solitary genius which offer a false escape from the burdens of craft, the miseries of credentialed professionalism, and the mockeries of creative entrepreneurship. Of course, value creators desperately struggling and failing to find other value creators will undoubtedly be tempted by the lures of solitary genius, but they should feel no shame in being tempted and in struggling with this temptation. Indeed, being tempted by the lures of solitary genius should be a badge of honor, an indicator that you are a value creator. The lures of solitary genius are the value creator's great vulnerability, yes, but there is no shame in being vulnerable. To the contrary, recognizing the lures of the solitary genius as a vulnerability and speaking honestly of and to this vulnerability in one's art is one sure way for a value creator to signal to other value creators that they are seeking fellow travelers.

Going further, it is important that the value creator not only seek fellow travelers but also seek to organize for mutual-aid with fellow travelers. Given that organizing for mutual-aid is extremely difficult, the value creator must make art that, in some way shape or form, brushes up against the difficulties that they face when organizing for mutual-aid. This is not at all to suggest that the value creator must make organizing for mutual-aid into the central focus of their art but, rather, that the value creator's work must make traces of such material difficulties into features of their art.

Put negatively, I believe that value creators with flailing careers and unmarketable brands should not keep up appearances to the contrary. Artists who aren't value creators will endeavor to erase unseemly traces of their everyday struggles from their art in order to save face in front of "refined audiences", or "professional organizations", or "social networks". In doing so, artists maintain the illusion that aristocracies, meritocracies, and markets can serve artists, and they cover up the fact that aristocracies, meritocracies, and markets make artists serve them and break artists that do not serve them. The fact that one cannot cut it as a master artisan, or a credentialed professional, or a creative entrepreneur is nothing to be ashamed of as a value creator but, rather to the contrary, it is another badge of honor, another good indicator that one is a value creator. Recognizing this inability and speaking honestly of and to this inability in one's art is a sure way for one to signal to other value creators that one is seeking fellow travelers with whom one can organize for mutual-aid.

In aesthetic terms, what all of this means is that the value creator must embrace the aesthetic of roughness in their art. The masterworks that the master artisan endeavors to create are never rough because they must be refined to the satisfaction of their aristocratic and priestly patrons. The career defining works that the credentialed professional endeavors to create are never rough because they must either meet or set the standards for best practices. The brand promoting work that the creative entrepreneur endeavors to create will use refinement, professionalism, and roughness as gimmicks, as cunning devices to increase the marketability of their brand, as such they may be rough in their design, but their roughness is a marketing ploy. Only the value creator's works are unrefined and unprofessional and unmarketable in their roughness. This does not mean, however, that the value creator's works are ugly! Quite to the contrary, the value creator's work *feels* beautiful to the value creator in spite of its being unrefined, unprofessional, and unmarketable.

Indeed, the key word here is "feels". The self-conscious value creator only becomes a value creator because the conventions of refinement, professionalism, and marketability do not align with their feelings about beauty. Indeed, the self-conscious value creator could be defined as the artist who expresses, in and through their art, the manner in which their own feelings about beauty deviate from the conventions of refinement, professionalism, and marketability. The self-conscious value creator refuses to keep up the appearance of being refined, professional, or marketable whenever and wherever doing so means smothering their feelings about beauty. Going further, the value creator's fellow travelers are those who share the value creator's feelings about beauty. Indeed, the reason why value creators form bands of fellow travelers and organize for mutual-aid is to prevent the conventions of refinement, professionalism, and marketability from smothering their shared feelings about beauty.

To embrace the aesthetic of roughness, then, is to embrace one's own feelings about beauty over the conventions of refinement, professionalism, and marketability. In Japanese philosophy the term for such an aesthetic of roughness is wabi-sabi (侘寂). The Japanese term wabi (侘) could be translated as "close to nature", or "exposed to the elements", and the term sabi (寂) could be translated "perishing" or "withered". Indeed, one might say that the value creator's an aesthetic of roughness creates exposed-and-perishing beauties lacking in refinement, professionalism, and marketability.

Value creators can only learn of one another in one of two ways: through personal acquaintance or through their reputation for showing talent in spite of being unrefined, unprofessional, and unmarketable. The value creator in search of fellow travelers dares to show their unrefined work to refined audiences, dares to show their unprofessional work to professional audiences, and dares to put their unmarketable work up for sale on the market. In doing so, the value creator seeks to unsettle refined, professional, and popular audiences with exposed-and-perishing beauties, hoping to generate rumor, speculation, and talk that could reach the ears of other value creators. It also follows that value creators attend closely to rumor, speculation, and talk of other unrefined, unprofessional, and unmarketable artists, hoping to learn of and seek out others whose exposed-and-perishing beauties are complementary to theirs.

I will leave off here because I have little more to offer. In summation, let me conclude this text with two bold propositions and a brief note on what these propositions mean for me as an artist.

First, I propose that every artist has a political economic ideology, a dream of what the artist's role in society should be, and every artist can be characterized, in terms of their political economic ideology, as either a conservative, a nihilist, a social progressive, a capitalist, or an autonomist.

- *The conservative dreams of becoming a master artisan and dreams of the aristocracies and priesthoods that would support their art.*
- *The nihilist dreams of becoming a solitary genius and dreams of "transcending" all communities and customs.*
- *The social progressive dreams of art-making as a respectable profession and dreams of receiving awards, honors, and offices.*
- *The capitalist dreams of making and breaking markets as a creative entrepreneur with a hot and profitable brand.*
- *The autonomist dreams of becoming a value creator and organizing for mutual-aid with fellow travelers.*

Second, I want to propose that the political economic ideology of an artist is part and parcel of the allure of their art.

- *The allures of the craftsmanship of the master artisan are the allures of conservatism.*

- *The allures of the transcendence of the solitary genius are the allures of nihilism.*

- *The allures of the expert technique of the credentialed professional are the allures of progressivism.*

- *The allures of the gimmicks of the creative entrepreneur are the allures of capitalism.*

- *The allures of the exposed-and-perishing beauties of the value creator are the allures of autonomism.*

Let me be clear here: there is no shame in succumbing to any one of these allures. To the contrary, there is only ever self-knowledge to be had in recognizing and speaking honestly of and to one's own susceptibility to these different allures. I am advocating for the figure of the value creator in this text, yes, but I believe that an artist should only ever become a value creator if they have strong feelings about beauty that are smothered by the conventions of refinement, professionalism, and marketability. Indeed, I believe that there is no sense in resisting the conventions of refinement, professionalism, and marketability unless one has strong feelings about beauty that compel one to resist.

In order to express my own feelings about beauty as a value creator, I have chosen, for myself and for myself alone, to resist the allures of conservatism, nihilism, progressivism, and capitalism and to devote myself to the allures of autonomism. I cannot do this effectively, however, unless I know the allures of conservatism, nihilism, progressivism, and capitalism for myself, and unless I learn how to resist these allures for myself. In order to embrace the allures of autonomism above all other allures, I have, with great care and deliberateness, endeavored to expose myself to the allures of conservatism, nihilism, progressivism, and capitalism, and I have endeavored to learn how neutralize their effects on me. Ay, and this learning process is what I have come to call my "sentimental education" as a value creator.